→ The last word on English

ENGLISH

Virgin

GCSE PASS

GCSE PASS

Frank Fitzsimons

Virgin BOOKS

VIRGIN REVISION GUIDE POWERED BY *Letts*

Contents

Virgin Help Section

Welcome to *Virgin GCSE English Revision Guide*. This unique pocket guide is designed to help your revision and boost your knowledge as you prepare for your GCSEs.

A team of revision experts has created this book to help you save time, avoid exam stress and make sure you get the best possible result. Here's how it works ....

Exam survival

Our expert advice on how to survive your exams will get you started; help you plan an effective revision programme; give you top tips on how to remember the key information; test your progress and reveal how best to survive the actual exams.

All you need to know

The information in this book is based on the core topics within the **Key Stage 4 National Curriculum** and **all GCSE exam specifications**. However, unlike textbooks or other revision guides it gives you **exactly what you need to know – and no more**.

The book is divided into eight clear sections. Each section contains all the specific topics you need to know to guarantee GCSE success.

Learn fast

Because each topic is presented on a single page, you can zoom in on the really essential information straight away. Start with the **Key Fact** at the top of the page, get to grips with the detail underneath and make sure you check out the **Grade Booster** comment before you test your knowledge on the opposite page.

Testing time

You've just read it, but do you know it? Well here's how to find out. Use the **Question Bank** to see if you really know your stuff. Check the answer section in the back of the book and if you got all the questions right, move on. If not, read the information again to see if you missed anything, then try again. Remember to revisit the Question Banks from time to time to make sure that the information has really sunk in.

Keeping your score

At the back of the book you will find a **Scoring Grid** where you can keep tabs on your progress. Keep your scores as you work through the book and see if you can spot any patterns emerging. For example, did you get more correct answers in the Shakespeare section? Then maybe you need to focus your learning on the Punctuation and Spelling and Poetry sections. **Remember, these are your results – use them to get even better!**

And there's more

Want to find out more? Well help is at hand. We have included a **glossary** of key English words and easy-to-understand definitions plus a list of useful **websites** that will help improve your knowledge and understanding.

Don't know where to start? Can't remember the key information? Worried about sitting the exam? Read on and get your questions answered.

You already know more than you think

The fact is that you've probably already encountered the key information you need for success at GCSE. Over a two-year period, you'll have been taught all of the core topics on your GCSE specification and your teachers will have explained the course structure and how it's examined. You'll have done a fair few homeworks, tests and no doubt some form of coursework. All of this counts and shouldn't be underestimated. All you need to do in the run-up to your GCSE exams is to revisit the information, bring it to the forefront of your mind and programme it into your memory.

Make a plan

Use your class notes and put them into a **logical order**. You'll soon build up an idea of the topics you have to revise and whether you're missing any key areas. If you're still unsure about certain areas of the course, check the relevant sections in this book or ask your teachers – that's what they're there for!

Work out the time you have available before the exams and exactly what needs to be revised. **Be realistic** – don't kid yourself that you'll do 8 hours of revision every day for 3 months. You have to eat, sleep, exercise and have a life too! It may be a relief to know that short bursts of revision, say about 30 minutes at a time, followed by a break are the most effective. A **manageable plan** covering all topics and setting a realistic number of hours for revision each week is the way forward.

From time to time go back and **revisit topics** that you have already revised. This will help you check your progress and also it will lock the information in your **long-term memory**.

Finally, it may sound obvious but don't forget the importance of noting the dates of all your exams. This will affect what you revise and when, not to mention making sure that you turn up on the right days!

Top revision techniques

There are several proven revision techniques to help you remember information more easily. None of these memory-boosting techniques are difficult to grasp, but everyone is different and some may work better for you than others. Try them all and find the method that suits you best.

For most students this means making your revision as **ACTIVE** as possible. For example, simply reading pages and pages may not make the information sink in. Why not use the same system that we have used in this book: read a page of information, write some questions, have a short break and then test yourself.

In the same way, try some of these techniques to trigger your memory whilst revising:

■ Try condensing your notes into short **revision cards**. You will learn as you go and you will build up a great library of Key Fact cards. Choose key words rather than writing full sentences. Break up the text with bullet points or numbers. Use a highlighter pen or underlining to emphasise the most important words. For instance, you could produce cards on pairs of 'Poems or Texts From Other Cultures' and note key themes and ideas that are found in both texts.

■ Using **different colours** will help the brain store and recall information. Try writing in up to four different colours, but try to be consistent; for example, themes could be red, characters blue, imagery green, etc.

■ **Be visual** – use drawings and labelled diagrams. A well-labelled diagram is an excellent way of recording information on a revision card. Diagrams should be kept very simple so they can be memorised and reproduced during the exam. This is great for remembering themes that link groups of poems or for characterisation, plots, themes and imagery of novels, etc.

■ **Idea maps, flow charts** and **spider diagrams**. Simple flow charts and idea maps link information together, especially where there is a process or sequence of events. A few words in boxes joined by arrows are all that is required. For example, a simple process may be shown as *'insert cash card → key in PIN → select service required → key in amount → press Accept → take card → take money'*. This method would be ideal for planning exam answers for Paper 1: **Writing to Argue, Persuade or Advise** and Paper 2: **Writing to Inform, Explain or Describe**.

- Drawing **humorous cartoons** makes revising more fun, and information easier to recall. To remember different aspects of imagery such as, say, metaphors, try drawing them. In the metaphor *Juliet is the sun* from 'Romeo and Juliet', you could draw Juliet's smiling face as the sun.

- Make up **rhymes** and **mnemonics** to remember key facts. This is a very powerful way of learning and recalling information. A simple mnemonic technique uses the first letters of words to recall lists, spellings and essay structure for poetry. For example, STRIDE: Subject, Theme, Rhythm, Imagery, Diction and Evaluation.

- **Repeat facts** out loud or why not try recording them onto a tape. You can then listen to them in different situations, e.g. waiting for a bus, doing the washing up, on the toilet! You could define terms such as 'emotive language' and recount various persuasive techniques and presentational devices used in texts.

- Try **testing** a classmate, a parent or a friend. We all love a quiz and asking questions is a great way of boosting your memory. Try defining literary terms, problem spellings, questions to identify types of texts and writing (writing to persuade, inform, entertain) etc.

The more your revision involves you *doing* something rather than simply reading, and the more visual it is, the more information you will find you retain.

- *Test yourself*

  It may sound corny, but 'practice really does make perfect'. As soon as you feel confident enough, you should attempt some practice questions. Try to familiarise yourself with the style of exam questions by *highlighting the key words in the question*. Get into the habit of planning your response before you actually start writing and then checking that your answer stays relevant as you write.

  The thing *not* to do with practice questions is to attempt them before you have revised. Learn your stuff *first* and then test yourself. You will soon see the progress you have made or be able to identify any areas that you find particularly difficult.

The big day

If you've worked hard studying and revising in the run-up to your GCSEs, do yourself one last favour and make sure you **don't panic** in the exam.

Very few people enjoy sitting exams, however everyone can make the experience less stressful by remembering the following exam techniques.

- **Read the instructions on the exam paper.** This is obvious, but really, really important. Take particular notice of the time allowed for the exam and the number of questions you are asked to attempt. Make sure you do this for every subject and every paper.

- **Pace yourself** through the exam. Read each question carefully and underline the key words to help focus and plan your answers. Remember to check the marks available for each question and to allocate your time accordingly.

- **Stay calm** no matter what the paper throws at you. Whilst it is advisable to attempt every question, you can always leave a difficult question until the end and come back to it once you have finished the rest of the paper.

- Finally, leave some time to **check through your answers**. Don't be tempted to cross out and change lots of answers in the last five minutes of the exam, rather use this time to check that your writing is legible, your spelling is accurate and that you've done the best you can.

Good luck!

We hope you find this book useful – and enjoy using it. GCSE exams are important and can be stressful, but if you prepare properly and do your best, you will succeed. Remember, once the exams are over … well, we'll leave all that to you!

English Language: the Course

> *At first glance the course can seem a bit complicated. But what's listed below, is what it all comes down to.*

English is assessed through four main skills. These are:

- speaking
- listening
- reading (with understanding)
- writing.

There are several exam boards and the order in which they examine these skills may vary, but the courses that they offer usually boil down to this:

1 **Orals** (20%) – three orals: a single, a paired and a group oral.

2 **Reading** (10%) – three assignments: a Shakespeare play; a comparison of two texts, *one of which must be written in prose before 1914 by a recognised author in the National Curriculum*; and a media assignment that is examined for both reading and writing.

3 **Writing** (10%) – again, this includes your media piece and an assignment on *either* original or personal writing.

Your coursework is therefore worth 40% of your final mark.

In your final exams, the breakdown is as follows:

- **Reading** (30%) – prepared texts (poems or prose 15%) and unseen texts (informative or persuasive texts 15%).

- **Writing** (30%) – writing to inform, explain or describe (15%) and writing to argue, persuade or advise (15%).

The final exams count for 60% of your final mark.

GRADE BOOSTER

Try to meet the deadlines that your teachers set for coursework assignments. Then you'll avoid putting yourself under unnecessary stress.

Question Bank 1

1   What are the four main skills examined in GCSE English Language?

    ....

2   Your three orals account for how much of your final mark?

    a   10%   ☐

    b   20%   ☐

    c   30%   ☐

3   What are the three assignments examined in reading and understanding?

    ....

4   What is the important instruction for the comparative reading assignment?

    ....

5   Your final exams are worth what percentage of the marks?

    ....

6   List the six skills examined in the writing sections of your final exams.

    ....

    ....

    ....

Speaking and Listening

Speaking and Listening accounts for 20% of your final score and it is a fairly easy way to build up your marks. Good grades here could make the difference between a D and a C or even better.

Your teacher will set you a minimum of three orals.

Your grades will then be added up and then divided by three to get your final oral grade.

You will be asked to do:

■ a **single** oral in which you'll speak on a topic on your own

■ a **paired** oral that you will prepare with a partner

■ a **group** oral either as a small group or with your whole class.

Remember that you will be assessed on your ability to:

■ explain, describe or narrate

■ explore, analyse or imagine

■ discuss, argue or persuade.

One set of criteria will be used in each of the orals until all three sets of skills have been covered. *Sometimes orals cover skills in more than one set of criteria.*

It is useful to keep a brief record of how your orals went. You can record what you did and make a note on how you can improve.

GRADE BOOSTER

If you have a bad oral, don't despair. You can do more than three orals and have higher grades substituted for lower ones.

Question Bank 2

True or false?

1 You need to do three orals.

   ....

2 You can do more than three orals.

   ....

3 You need to include all three sets of criteria in each oral.

   ....

4 Each oral will test a separate set of criteria.

   ....

5 More than one set of criteria may be used in an oral.

   ....

6 The orals account for 30% of your final grade.

   ....

7 You can get away with only doing two orals.

   ....

Speaking and Listening: Grading Criteria

> *Don't be put off by having to talk in front of others, especially when you know that you will be graded for your talk. Your teachers know you and they'll be trying to give you the highest grade you deserve.*

How to get high grades in speaking and listening

When you speak your teachers will be trying to answer these questions:

- Can you speak with **confidence** and **fluency** on a selected topic without being hampered by notes?

- Is there a **clear structure** in your talk? Does your talk have a beginning, a middle and an end?

- Are you using an **appropriate register**? That is, using the correct tone of voice and matching your tone to your audience.

- How well can you use **standard English and grammar**? You must use standard English for formal talks and avoid using your local dialect.

- Are you able to **listen with sensitivity** and **respond in the same manner**? Can you carry forward the points and ideas of others?

- Are you able to listen and respond to **a range of complex speech**?

- Can you **sustain a point of view** in a discussion (argument), initiate speech or manage the points of others?

- Can you make **thought-provoking points** with wide-ranging vocabulary, irony, rhetorical questions, etc.?

GRADE BOOSTER

Don't let nerves get the better of you. Show that you're a good listener and turn-taker when speaking.

Question Bank 3

1 Why is it important to keep notes to a minimum when you speak?

....

2 What is 'register'?

....

3 What type of English should you use when giving a formal talk?

....

4 Why is it important to listen?

....

5 When you are sustaining a point of view, what are you doing?

....

6 What is a rhetorical question?

....

Standard English

Standard English and your ability to speak it is perhaps the skill that teachers are listening out for most. After reading this page you should have no problems recognising this dialect.

Standard English is formal English. It is the dialect of business, power, instruction and authority.

Standard English originated in the East Midlands many centuries ago and this **dialect** gradually became the standard form of English used by influential people across Britain. Today, this **variety of speech** is used by a range of people from lawyers to office staff who have to use **a formal style of English** to conduct business, instruct others or deal with people they do not know.

When you speak it you fully pronounce all your words and deliberately avoid abbreviated words or local words and phrases.

This dialect is a standardised form of English with slight variations in the many countries where English is spoken. Its speakers habitually use it to understand each other wherever English is spoken, from the United States to Australia.

Another important reason for its use is politeness. It would be silly to speak in your local dialect to someone from another part of the UK when they might struggle to understand your meaning.

Have you noticed that the text on this page is written quite **formally** using **standard English**?

Question Bank 4

1   Examine the four spoken sentences below.

Which are in standard English?

a   'My Dear Larrds an Membas of de Dread House'   ☐

b   ' Good evening. This is the ten o'clock news'.   ☐

c   'Thor wes yence a toon caaled Newcastle-on-Tyne an' this
toon wes full o' moggies.'   ☐

d   'Rarely in the field of human conflict was so much owed to so few'. ☐

2   Who uses standard English and why do they use it?

    ....

3   How does standard English aid speakers from across the globe?

    ....

4   Give another reason why standard English is used.

    ....

5   In which region did standard English originate?

    ....

Local Dialects

Even if people are sometimes unaware of it, almost everyone has a regional accent and speaks more than one dialect. ***A person's dialect is an important part of their identity.***

Local dialect is informal or casual English.

This is a relaxed form of speech that you use with your friends and family. There is no problem about dropping your Ts and Hs in your local dialect. You will also use local turns of phrase with the full knowledge that the person you are talking to understands everything that you're saying.

In fact, if you use the more formal standard English in friendly situations you run the risk of being thought of as cold and strange. You would hardly say to your best friend, 'Let us visit the cinema' when 'Let's go to the pictures' or 'Let's go and see a film' would be more natural.

There are many dialects spoken in the UK, including:

- Estuary English

- Liverpudlian

- Geordie

- Jamaican

- Glaswegian.

Can you think of any others? Identify your own local dialect and why you use it.

GRADE BOOSTER

In oral assignments, try to use the best standard English that you can and avoid slipping into your local dialect. That's the way to higher grades.

Question Bank 5

True or false?

1   Most of the UK population only use one dialect.

    ....

2   Using your local dialect is a formal way of speaking English.

    ....

3   You use local dialects with your friends and family because it is a casual and
    friendly way of speaking to them.

    ....

4   Cockney is a dialect.

    ....

5   You should speak in your local dialect when you:

    a   give formal talks ....

    b   talk with strangers ....

    c   answer the phone in an office ....

    d   read the news on television. ....

Accent

> It may at first seem difficult to tell someone's accent apart from their dialect. All you need to remember is that a person's **dialect** consists of **local words and phrases**, and that **accent** is the **sound of a person's voice** as they **pronounce** those words.

A speaker's accent is the *sound* they make as they pronounce their vowels and consonants.

Some well-known regional accents in the British Isles include:

- West Country
- Irish
- Welsh
- Scottish
- Northern.

Accents also help you to distinguish people's origins from different countries and regions within their countries. For instance, you might recognise an Irish accent, but you might also be able to tell whether the speaker is from the North or South and even which region of Ireland, such as Kerry or Dublin.

Like dialect, accent is a mark of our identity. It helps others know where we are from.

However, there is one accent that is difficult to place as **all its speakers sound the same wherever they are from.** This is picked up in many independent schools, for example, or from parents and it is called **Received Pronunciation (RP).** You'll hear this accent spoken by some BBC broadcasters, the Royal Family and many privileged members of society.

So what is an accent? It is the distinctive sounds that a person makes when they speak either in their local dialect or in standard English. For example, a Scottish newsreader will use standard English, but speak with a Scottish accent.

GRADE BOOSTER

Make a brief chart with clear headings of all the accents you hear in your school or from your family, neighbours and friends.

Question Bank 6

1 What does RP mean?

   a Royal Person ☐

   b Received Pronunciation ☐

   c Repeat ☐

2 What is an accent?

   a the words and phrases that a speaker uses ☐

   b a dialect ☐

   c the sound that a person makes when they speak ☐

3 Which accent makes it difficult to tell where the speaker is from?

   a American ☐

   b RP ☐

   c Southern ☐

4 Where does an accent identify us as coming from?

   a a region or country ☐

   b a family ☐

   c a suburb ☐

5 Which of these accents tells us that the speaker is not from the UK?

   a Cockney ☐

   b Liverpudlian ☐

   c Australian ☐

How to Plan a Talk

For starters, work out a brief plan for each oral because this will improve the structure as well as your fluency and self-confidence.

Remember that your teacher will test *one* of the following sets of skills when you speak:

- explain, describe or narrate
- explore, analyse or imagine
- discuss, argue or persuade.

What to do

- Focus on the **title** of your talk to keep notes relevant.
- **Research** your information. See experts, visit libraries, search on the Internet, etc.
- Plan the **structure** of your talk. You'll need a clear introduction, main body and conclusion.
- Prepare any **props or handouts** and think about where you might use them in your talk.

Planning methods

Spider diagrams and **brainstorms** are excellent ways of planning your talk with a few simple images. Write the key idea in a circle in the middle of a large sheet of paper. Then write other key words in circles, with lines showing how the ideas are linked.

Using cards when you speak

- Write key points and phrases in large print on postcard-sized cards.
- Prepare your cards in the correct logical order for the talk.
- As you go through each point, place that card at the bottom of the pack.

If you use this system be careful that you do not write too much on the cards.

Practise your talk with a friend. Alternatively, try your talk in front of a mirror. Work out any unusual or topic-specific words.

GRADE BOOSTER

Ask a friend to listen to you, and note any lapses from standard English and grammar. Get another pair of ears on your side.

Question Bank 7

1 Give **one** of the three sets of criteria that teachers will use to set your talk.

....

....

2 Why is it important to plan your talk?

....

3 Give three sources of information for talks.

....

....

....

4 Identify one method of planning your talk.

....

5 How can you practise your talk?

....

Presenting Orals

If the thought of speaking in front of others makes you feel sick, remind yourself that your teacher is only looking for what you can do well.

Remember the purpose of your talk and adapt your speech to your audience.

Look over the grading criteria mentioned in the previous pages.

When you speak:

- **Stand up,** if appropriate, take a few deep breaths and try to appear relaxed and confident.

- **Vary the pitch** of your voice. Avoid speaking in a monotone.

- **Use standard English** as fluently as you can in **your own accent.**

- **Speak in the correct register.** (You would speak to other students with a different tone of voice than you would if you were talking to an MP.)

- **Take questions** at appropriate points in your speech.

- **Listen carefully** to what others say and try to further your topic.

- **Take turns** when speaking in a group and ensure that your comments are relevant.

- **Use body language and gestures** when you speak.

- **Establish eye contact with your audience.** Look several members of your audience in the eye to draw them into what you are saying.

- Smile, use your hands and move about. Do anything to **hold your audience's interest.** (But don't distract them!)

- Try to **end your talk on a positive note** with maybe a joke or an anecdote. Avoid fizzling out with something like, 'That's it'.

GRADE BOOSTER

Why not self-assess your own talk? Think about what you did well and note what you need to do to improve.

Question Bank 8

1   How can you avoid speaking in a monotone?

   a by using the same tone and pitch of voice ☐

   b by varying your pitch and tone ☐

   c by sounding like a robot ☐

2   Which dialect should you use?

   a Standard English ☐

   b Geordie ☐

   c Estuary English ☐

3   What is the other main skill that you need to show?

   a the ability to shout ☐

   b that you can cut in on others ☐

   c that you can listen and take turns when speaking ☐

4   Which of the following aspects of body language should you use?

   a eye contact ☐

   b staring ☐

   c looking at the ground as you speak ☐

5   How can you end your talk on a high note?

   a By stuttering, 'That's all for now folks.' ☐

   b With a joke or a brief quotation. ☐

   c By laughing out loud. ☐

Original Writing: Non-Fiction

> *Teachers often set this assignment early in your course to build confidence and get you off to a flying start. These skills are a must for the final exams as well.*

Non-fiction means not made up.

The type of assignments that you may be asked to write about include:

- **autobiography** (a period of your life, a description of a day, a memorable holiday or visit, etc.)
- a **discussion** of a topic or an issue
- an **explanation** of an interesting picture from a magazine or a newspaper
- a **description** of a building or a **process** of how to do something, etc.

You need to consider **three** areas:

1 **audience** – the people who will read your work
2 **purpose** – are you setting out to explain and describe, persuade, instruct, advise, etc.?
3 **content** – your thoughts, feelings and relevant information in some detail

To get a C to A* grade you will need to:

- **Research** your topic.
- Produce an **appropriate** and **organised** assignment.
- Be **compelling** and give a **convincing** account of a real experience.
- Use **standard written forms** in a **realistic** manner.
- Be both **detailed** and **concise**.
- Match your **tone** and **language** to your **audience**.
- Show control over your writing by using **appropriate punctuation, word choices and sentence structure**.
- Use **wide-ranging vocabulary** with **hardly any errors** in syntax, spelling and punctuation.

GRADE BOOSTER

Find out how to use semi-colons (;) and colons (:) in your writing. Examiners love them! (See pages 178 and 180.)

Question Bank 9

1 What does non-fiction mean?

   ....

2 True or false?

   a A short story can count as non-fiction.

      ....

   b A detailed description of a day in your life is non-fiction.

      ....

   c Novels can be called non-fiction.

      ....

3 What are the three main points that you must consider for every
   piece of writing?

   ....

4 Give one example of a purpose for writing.

   ....

5 How can you achieve control in your writing?

   ....

Planning Personal Writing

Let's start by looking at the steps needed to build a writing plan for a non-fiction assignment.

Every piece of writing must be planned.

Writing that is planned is always more detailed and structured than writing that is unplanned.

Try the following steps when you plan your assignment on non-fiction:

1 **Think about your topic** and **consider your target audience.** Your topic's purpose and the audience that you want to reach will help shape your written **form**: a letter, essay, pamphlet, diary, article, etc.

2 **Research your topic.** Think about where you may find your information: libraries, the Internet, knowledgeable people, etc.

3 **Make notes on single sides of paper** and then number your pages. It's easier to find notes that way. Why not plan with brainstorms or spider diagrams?

4 **Read over your notes and plan your assignment on a single sheet of paper.** Then number your points and ideas in the order that you want to write about them.

5 **Write the title at the top of your first draft to keep you focused.** Think about the best way of expressing your ideas by tinkering with your sentences.

6 **Produce your best draft.** Remember to **proofread your work** for errors in punctuation, expression, etc.

GRADE BOOSTER

Make sure that your piece of writing has linking words and sentences to tie your ideas together. Think of these as signposts for an audience to follow your ideas.

Question Bank 10

1 Why must every piece of writing be planned?

   ....

2 Fill in the gaps.

   a When you consider a topic or issue you need to consider your target

      ....

   b You also need to think about your .... because this is

      what you are setting out to achieve.

   c The .... of your work should be appropriate for your

      audience and it can range from letters to essays.

3 Why should you make notes on only one side of paper?

   ....

4 How many drafts do you need?

   ....

5 What must you do after completing each draft of your work?

   ....

How to Plan an Essay

This causes anxiety for a lot of students, but once you've studied this page planning essays should be much less of a problem.

The key to writing good essays is planning.

Try to do the following:

1 **Examine the question's key words and phrases** to get a clear idea of what is being asked of you. You are going to construct an argument.

2 **Read through the text or the appropriate part of the text and make notes under clear headings** suggested by **key words and phrases**. For example, if you are asked for your views on 'Which character is most to blame for the tragedy of *Macbeth*?' you could make notes on separate pages for **key characters** such as Macbeth, Lady Macbeth and the witches.

3 Another way of making notes is to **brainstorm or make spider diagrams** of essay plans by writing key points around essay questions on large sheets of paper and drawing lines to show how the points are linked.

4 **Look through your notes and plan your essay on a single sheet of paper.** After your introduction you will need to **plan three or four main stages of your argument.** Each stage should have a number of closely-related points backed by page numbers for **quotations**. You must use **evidence** from the text to **support your arguments**.

GRADE BOOSTER

Remember that exam essays need planning too, even if it's only putting down a few main points and numbering them to help your structure.

Question Bank 11

1　What are the main things to look for to get a deeper understanding
of essay questions?

....

2　Identify two graphic ways of making notes.

....

....

3　How many stages should you have in your argument/essay?

....

4　What should you include in your essay to support your arguments?

....

5　How should you pull together your notes in the final plan for your essay?

....

Writing an Essay

> *Don't put off writing essays! Once you've got to grips with the introduction you'll be surprised how easy it is to keep writing.*

Your introduction

- If some **historical context** (ideas and attitudes when the text was written) is required, mention this briefly early in your essay. However, these points can also appear later on.
- **Begin with a topic sentence** (key sentence) which sums up your main argument with three or four main points. Then expand them into a paragraph. Your opening paragraph could look like a conclusion!

For example, if you were writing an essay on 'Which character is most to blame for the tragedy of *Macbeth*?' you could introduce the historical context with:

Shakespeare wrote his play just as James I became King in 1603...

You could begin with your main argument with:

There are several characters who could be blamed for the 'tragedy'; these include: Lady Macbeth, the witches and Macbeth himself...

The main body of your essay

- Remember to prove each point with **evidence** (brief quotations) from the text and **comment on your evidence**.
- **Make arguments flow in paragraphs** by using an appropriate range of connectives (linking words and phrases).

Your conclusion

- Your final paragraph should have a tone of finality (it sounds as if you are ending).
- Sum up your main arguments in relation to the essay question.
- If possible, show an awareness of alternative interpretations and arguments.

GRADE BOOSTER

Read your work aloud and listen for the flow and sense of your arguments. Check for errors in punctuation.

Question Bank 12

Fill in the gaps.

1 The ideas and attitudes present when the text was written are known as the

....

2 The main sentence in a paragraph is known as a ....

sentence.

3 A good place to introduce a paragraph or so on a text's historical context is

near the .... of your essay.

4 Brief .... to support your points are needed as evidence when

writing about texts.

5 Try to comment on your quotations and relate them, where possible, to the

....

6 Aim to signpost your arguments for your readers by including

....

7 In your conclusion tell what you have learned by giving your

.... on the text.

How to Make Spider Diagrams

Spider diagrams are an easy and memorable way of making notes for any topic. Once you've read this page your note-making may never be the same again!

Spider diagrams can be made for any topic. You can make them for:

- **characters** (their description, motivation, what they say, what others say about them, etc.)
- **themes** (ideas or messages in texts)
- **imagery** (similes and metaphors and what they suggest)
- **mood** and **atmosphere** (how it is created through description and imagery)
- **dramatic tension** (how it is created in scenes of plays, etc.)
- **plots** (outlines of stories).

Preparation

Before you start writing, **examine key words and phrases** in assignments and **re-read the relevant chapters or parts of texts**.

How to produce a spider diagram

1 Use a **pencil** and **white, unlined paper**, as this will speed your progress. Your most productive period will be the first five minutes.

2 **Begin around a main heading in the centre and work outwards.** Write the key words and ideas and circle them. The most important information should be in the centre and the least important around the edges.

3 Tape another page to sides or corners if you are running out of space. **Keep maps to a single, viewable piece of paper.**

4 **Link related ideas** with branches (lines) and images.

5 Work up your map later by adding **appropriate colours** and **detailed images** to make it memorable.

GRADE BOOSTER

Pictures and colours can help us memorise ideas and details. Why not use a simple spider diagram for your next oral?

Question Bank 13

1   What should you do before creating a spider diagram?

    ....

2   Identify an aspect of a text for which you could produce a spider diagram.

    ....

3   What do you need to produce a simple spider diagram?

    ....

4   When is the most creative period for a spider diagram?

    ....

5   How can you make your spider diagram memorable?

    ....

6   What should you do with related ideas in a spider diagram?

    ....

Connectives 1

This page should make essays and written assignments easier by giving you a bank of words and phrases which can act as signposts for points and arguments.

Words to help give examples and make points

You will already be using many of these words in your work. Broaden your range by including the *connectives* that you never use.

Adapt these words if necessary to suit your meaning.

To introduce examples

for example	for instance	as revealed by	such as	as an illustration of this
take the case of	to show that	thus	as with	evidently

To make additional points or add ideas

what is more	and	and then	also	again
furthermore	in addition	moreover	as well as	too

To argue

thus	consequently	because	hence	so we can see this	this suggests
so	as a result	therefore	since	it could be argued that	accordingly

To emphasise points

above all	in particular	especially	significantly	in fact
more importantly	indeed	notably	specifically	

Paragraphs also help organise ideas.

Paragraphs are **sections of writing** that help readers follow our meaning by breaking up texts for easy understanding. You need a **new paragraph** each time that you:

- change focus
- change the speaker
- introduce a different setting or place
- change the time within your story.

GRADE BOOSTER

Words such as 'moreover' and 'furthermore' are rarely found at GCSE level and will impress examiners if used correctly.

Question Bank 14

1 Write these words in the correct boxes

   a indeed, above all, in particular, most importantly

   b for instance, such as, as with, take the case of

   c what is more, furthermore, moreover, again

   d consequently, as a result, since, thus

   Words to introduce examples

   Words to argue and make points

   Words to add points or ideas

   Words that emphasise points

2 You need a new paragraph to signify a change of time, place, focus

   or ....

Connectives 2

Connectives can help writing to become more **structured, persuasive** or **analytical**. Connectives are especially useful for the wide-reading assignment where you'll have to **compare** two texts. Let's start with connectives that help put ideas in order.

Connectives for structure

then	first	second	third	next	eventually
subsequently	at last	at length	afterwards	so far	in the end

For exceptions

only if	unless	except (for)	save for

To persuade, analyse or give an opinion

of course	obviously		certainly	clearly	surely	evidently
infer	imply	deduce	propose			naturally
think	state	conclude	say	it seems/appears		

To contrast what is different

on the contrary	however	yet	the opposite	to turn to	whereas	despite this
alternatively	nevertheless	but	although	instead	still	in contrast

To compare what is the same

similarly	equally	also	compared with	likewise	in the same way

Words for conclusions

in brief	in summary	throughout	to sum up	to conclude	finally
in all	on the whole	overall	in the end	to recap	

Topic sentences and paragraphs

A topic sentence is the **main sentence** that identifies the **focus** of that paragraph. It is usually found at the start of a paragraph but it can be placed elsewhere within a paragraph.

GRADE BOOSTER

Remember that if you write your essays by hand, the first line of each new paragraph must be indented about 2 cm from the margin. There is no need to indent new paragraphs in word-processed essays.

Question Bank 15

1 If your essay title asks you to 'compare and contrast', what does this mean?

....

2 Identify the function of these words and phrases as words to either:

- ■ sum up [ ]
- ■ contrast [ ]
- ■ compare. [ ]

a whereas, however, although

b likewise, similarly, in the same way

c to sum up, to conclude, finally

3 What is a topic sentence?

....

4 Where in a paragraph are topic sentences often found?

....

5 What is a connective?

....

6 Do you need to indent new paragraphs in word-processed work?

....

Fiction: Original and Creative Writing

Most students enjoy this assignment; if your grade for it is higher than for your personal reading assignment then this grade can be submitted as your coursework assignment for writing.

Fiction is made-up writing.

The **key skills** are your ability to:

- **explore**
- **imagine**
- **entertain.**

Length

Most exam boards are happy with around 1000 words, but your piece can be longer or shorter. Don't let it go on too long, as it may then become unfocused.

Purpose and audience

You will secure a high mark if your piece:

- has clear aims with a specific purpose
- is appropriate for a specific audience
- is effectively written and convincing
- is concise.

To get a grade from C to A* you need to:

- Use a **varied range of sentences and vocabulary** to hold your audience's interest.
- Write in an **appropriate manner** and **genre**.
- Be **accurate with punctuation** and **logical with paragraphs**.
- Show **control over your expression and punctuation** to achieve effects.
- Show **clear settings** and **develop your characters**.
- Use **imagery** such as **metaphors and similes** effectively.
- Be conscious of **tone of voice** in words and sentences (should it be friendly, formal, etc.?)
- Be nearly **faultless** with **spelling and punctuation**.
- Have **flair** and **originality**.
- Be **elaborate** as well as **concise**.

GRADE BOOSTER

Why not read some good short stories and mark them against the criteria above? You'll find some at websites listed in the back of this book.

Question Bank 16

1 Can your original assignment be submitted for coursework instead of your personal writing assignment?

....

2 What are the three main skills for creative or original writing?

....

3 Fill in the gap.

Every piece of writing needs a clear purpose, should be written for a particular

.... and should be effectively written.

4 What is the average length expected for writing other than poetry?

....

5 Why is it a good idea to vary your vocabulary and punctuation?

....

6 What is 'control' in writing?

....

7 What is 'tone' in writing?

....

Ideas for Original Writing

> *Some people don't think that they're creative; after reading through the range of possibilities on this page you shouldn't be one of them.*

The assignment

Your teacher will set you an appropriate task. But there's no reason why you cannot submit an extra assignment drawn from the ideas set out below. Clear it with your teacher first.

Let's look at some things that you might write about. You could:

- Write a few **diary entries from a character who impressed you** in a novel or a short story.

- Write a **ballad** (a story poem) on a **topical issue** in the news. (If you choose this option, read a few ballads and find out how they are set out.)

- Write a short **horror story** with a twist in the tail (its ending).

- Write an **episode** or a few extra scenes for a **soap opera** from either a well-known soap or one that you've made up.

- Write a **brief play** using characters from a play that you have studied.

- Amuse and entertain an audience with **detailed descriptions of people or places**.

- Write an **extra chapter or scene** of a play that you've read.

- **Take two famous figures from history or characters from different texts** and imagine their conversation.

Most teachers welcome such assignments as long as it is all your own work.

GRADE BOOSTER

Remember to make two drafts, and proofread your work for clarity, relevance and punctuation.

Question Bank 17

1 Before you offer an assignment of your own, what must you do?

   ....

   ....

2 What kind of poems are ballads?

   ....

3 How should you try to end a story, especially a horror story?

   ....

4 What can you try with a soap opera?

   ....

5 When you complete any piece of writing, what must you always do?

   ....

   ....

Planning: Plot, Character and Setting

> *Once you are aware of the basic ingredients of stories, planning is quite easy. Let's look at three important ingredients.*

Plot

A plot is the outline of your story. Plots can come from almost anything. They could arise from:

- a character getting into trouble, involving **suspense**
- the **traits of a character** (friendly, mean, naïve, selfish, etc.)
- a **title** or perhaps even the **first sentence** or so from a famous novel
- an **unusual viewpoint** such as a baby's or a parrot's
- an **unusual setting** such as a swamp or a place in the past or future.

Character

In short stories, **keep characters to a minimum.** It's a good idea to **create a profile** for each character, as this will help you portray them **realistically**. Think about their appearance, job, habits, ambitions, fears, likes and dislikes, etc.

Setting

You need to think about **where and when** you set your story. Do you want to set your story in the past, present or future? What details will you need to **make your setting convincing**?

GRADE BOOSTER

Build tension in your story by making your plot come to a *climax*. This is when things come to a head and a crisis occurs. It's the highpoint of any story.

Question Bank 18

True or false?

1 A plot is the setting of a story.

....

2 A plot can be made out of an unusual setting.

....

3 An interesting title or the first lines of a good book could start you on the path
   to a story.

....

4 You do not need to clear assignments with your teacher.

....

5 You should try to keep to no more than two or three important characters.

....

6 The setting means a time and place in a story.

....

7 Lots of detail will make your story convincing.

....

Planning: More Story Ingredients

Planning a really good story means adding several ingredients. Let's take a look at five more vital ingredients for success.

There are five more elements of your story to consider: narrative stance, structure, genre, time-scale and a strong ending.

1 Narrative stance

From whose point of view will you narrate your story? Is your story best told in the *first person* (from within the story, 'I') or *third person* (from outside the story, 'he' or 'she')?

2 Structure

Ensure that your story has **a clear beginning, middle and end**. You also need to consider your introduction. **A good hook at the beginning** will intrigue your audience and make them read on. This can be achieved through an unusual description of a **setting, character or incident**.

3 Genre (kind of story)

Select an appropriate genre for your story. This can be adventure, science fiction, romance, horror story, etc. There can also be subdivisions within genres such as tragi-comedy, comic-horror, etc.

4 Time-scale

You need to consider the **time-scale of your plot**. Will it be set over several hours or days? If you use time this way it is called **linear**. Or will you use flashbacks where **time moves forwards and backwards**. This is called **non-linear**.

5 Strong ending

Aim for a strong ending. You might have, for example, a **moral** for your tale. Another strong way to end a story is to include an **unexpected twist**.

> ### GRADE BOOSTER
> **Examine beginnings in stories and try to see what their *hooks* are. How do they grab the reader's attention? If a story has *suspense*, how is it achieved?**

Question Bank 19

1   If a first-person narrator tells the story, is the narrator speaking from within the story or outside of it?

   ....

2   Structure-wise, what must each story clearly have?

   ....

3   Briefly explain what 'genre' means.

   ....

4   If a story is written in a linear way, how is time used?

   ....

5   What does 'non-linear' mean?

   ....

6   Give two good ways of ending a story.

   ....

7   Where would you expect to see a 'hook' in a story?

   ....

8   What can a 'hook' be? ....

Creative Writing Skills 1

This is not as tricky as it seems. If you can manage two or more of the three skills discussed below you will improve the quality of your writing.

1 Diction (word choices)

The deliberate selection of words can create effects. For instance, the repeated use of a variety of religious words can give a hushed, respectful, and elevated feel to the description of a person or a place. In other words, **tone** can be created by carefully-chosen words.

2 Reversal of the expected word order

This can be a very effective device to use if you want to **emphasise** a character's actions, thoughts or feelings. For example, if you want to say, 'Jenny was shocked and cried after losing her boyfriend to her best friend, Anna;' you could try:

Shocked, Jenny cried after seeing Anna, her best friend, steal her boyfriend.

By putting 'her best friend' just before 'steal' Jenny's 'shock' is amplified.

3 Variation of sentences

You can **create effects** by **varying the lengths of your sentences**. Shorter sentences tend to be more dramatic and help convey characters' emotions or **build suspense**. Longer sentences are good for description and details when describing a **setting** or a **character**.

GRADE BOOSTER

Spend some time changing around your sentences and expressions; you'll be surprised at the results and at your grades!

Question Bank 20

1 What does 'diction' mean?

   a a form of dictation ☐

   b how a character pronounces their words ☐

   c the word choices that a writer makes in their prose or poetry ☐

2 What is tone influenced by?

   a how someone listens to another character ☐

   b the word choices that writers make ☐

   c songs sung by characters ☐

3 What does the reversal of the expected word order create?

   a no effect at all in writing ☐

   b an effect that can emphasise thoughts, feelings and actions ☐

   c a feeling of light-headedness ☐

4 What can varying the lengths of your sentences do?

   a send your readers to sleep ☐

   b help convey characters' emotions, actions and suspense ☐

   c confuse your readers ☐

5 What can longer sentences help to do?

   a produce suspense ☐

   b express a dramatic action ☐

   c produce descriptive passages for setting the scene or
describing a character ☐

Creative Writing Skills 2

> *Producing good, descriptive writing can seem challenging, but it isn't really very difficult. Let's start with looking at what description means. **Description means to set out something in words.***

Descriptive writing

Descriptive writing should have detailed sentences in which **adjectives** say more about **nouns** and **adverbs** qualify **verbs**.

*It was a **silvery, dark, winter's** night when Steve **unsteadily** walked along the **icy** pavement to Gemma's house.*

Use the five senses to make subjects and settings more **realistic. Metaphors and similes** (word-picture comparisons) can also give a sense of:

- sight
- taste
- touch
- smell.
- hearing

For example:

The children's blankets were as soft as cats' fur.

Use hints and suggestion rather than direct statement

It is a good idea to **suggest or hint at as much as possible** when building up details on characters and settings rather than making **direct statements**. This helps readers use their imagination. For example, instead of saying directly that a character felt afraid, we could say that the hairs on the back of their neck stood up.

How to write effective sentences

Tinker with sentences for improved expressiveness.

- The **end** of a sentence has most impact.
- The **beginning** is the next most important for impact.
- The **middle** is the least important part of the sentence for impact.

Look at this example from George Orwell's *Coming Up For Air*:
The idea really came to me the day I got my new false teeth.

> ### GRADE BOOSTER
> Don't get carried away and overdo description. Use metaphors and similes sparingly. Description should *complement* your plot – too much will slow the pace of your story down and make it sound stilted.

Question Bank 21

1 What does 'description' mean?

....

2 Why is it a good idea to use one or more of the five senses in description?

....

3 List the five senses.

....

....

4 Why is it better to hint or suggest rather than make direct statements in description?

....

5 Which part of a sentence carries most impact?

....

6 Briefly explain the dangers of overdoing description.

....

Improve Your Expression 1

*A common area of difficulty in writing is expressing yourself clearly. Let's see why. **Brevity and clarity are essential for good expression.***

Unnecessary repetition of meaning

The use of words and phrases that merely repeat the meaning that has already been conveyed is known as a **tautology**. Look carefully at the underlined words below:

He spent five years in prison, where he planned his <u>vendetta</u> of <u>revenge</u>.

Adding the phrase 'of revenge' is unnecessary – the word 'vendetta' means revenge. Some writers strain verbs with **unnecessary word-reinforcement** and wrap them in '**dressing gowns**'. For example:

> <u>absolutely</u> and <u>completely</u>
>
> <u>wholly</u> understand
>
> Natalie was <u>thoroughly</u> mistaken in her accusations!

The last sentence has more force without the 'dressing gown'.

Brevity and clarity

The best way to say anything is often to use the fewest words possible. Avoid showy words and phrases and use simple ones instead. For example:

> blue in colour = blue
>
> in the majority of cases = usually
>
> owing to the fact that = since

If your readers can follow your intended meaning then your writing is clear. The writers of these **ambiguous** advertisements were not quite clear enough!

NOW IS YOUR CHANCE to have your ears pierced and get an extra pair to take home, too.

DOG FOR SALE Eats anything and is fond of children.

GRADE BOOSTER

Strike out any unnecessary words or phrases in your work and listen to the difference by reading your work aloud.

Question Bank 22

1 What does the word 'tautology' mean?

   ....

2 Rewrite the sentence below using the fewest words possible.

   Despite the fact that the football team did not play well they got on top of the
   situation and ran out worthy winners.

   ....

3 Identify the 'dressing gown' in the next sentence.

   His act was wholly unjustifiable.

   ....

4 Try to sum up the following phrases using one word.

   a *In the light of the fact that*   ....

   b *He is a man who*   ....

   c *At this juncture in time*   ....

5 These signs were spotted in offices. What's wrong with them?

   Would the person who took the step-ladder yesterday
   kindly bring it back or further steps will be taken. ....

   After the tea break, staff should empty the teapot
   and stand upside down on the draining board. ....

6 What does 'ambiguous' mean? If you're not sure, look it up in a dictionary.

   ....

Improve Your Expression 2

After you've read this page you'll have this topic – if you don't mind the cliché – all wrapped up. **Avoid clichés and overworked, informal words.**

Clichés

These are **worn-out expressions** that are 'well past their sell-by date' and have no force left in them. They are often ready-made phrases that were once fashionable metaphors and similes. There are hundreds of clichés in use – phrases that people write or say without thinking about whether an alternative would be more effective. Common examples include:

- *unveiled* (for new projects)
- *food for thought*
- *dead as a doornail*
- *shot himself in the foot*
- *as quick as a flash*

Overworked or weak, informal words

Try, if possible, to **avoid** words like these in your prose:

- *nice*
- *get/got*
- *totally*
- *a lot*
- *kind of*
- *actually*
- *basically*
- *in actual fact*

Most of these words are baggage and are too casual to be used in **formal writing**.

> ## GRADE BOOSTER
>
> The ability to use *appropriate vocabulary and phrasing* as well as a good knowledge of *punctuation* reveals your *control* in writing. Markers always reward such skills with high grades.

Question Bank 23

1 For each underlined phrase, choose an appropriate word or phrase to replace it from the list below.

   a <u>In many cases</u> boys achieved higher marks than girls. ....

   b <u>It has rarely been the case that</u> mistakes have been made. ....

   c <u>She is a woman who is</u> very ambitious. ....

   She is   Few   Many

2 What is a cliché? ....

3 Which of the following are well-known clichés?

   a *I'm over the moon*   ☐

   b *it's a piece of cake*   ☐

   c *pass like ships in the night*   ☐

   d *every parent's worst nightmare*   ☐

   e *cool as a cucumber*   ☐

   f *an emotional roller-coaster*   ☐

4 Tick the words that you use without thinking in your writing and avoid them in future!

   a amazing   ☐

   b awesome   ☐

   c definitely   ☐

   d interesting   ☐

   e strange   ☐

   f weird   ☐

   g situation   ☐

   h unbelievable   ☐

The Media Assignment

> The media assignment is one of the most interesting and easiest to do. Let's kick off by looking at what's expected from you. **Every exam board sets media tasks either for coursework or in the exams.**

You will be marked for **reading and writing skills**. In particular, you will be expected to **analyse, review and comment**.

Assignments and tasks can be drawn from: magazine adverts, radio and televisions adverts, articles, film scripts, scenes from films or any printed material published by the media.

High grades can be achieved if you:

■ Give **detailed points** and ideas.
■ Make **fine distinctions** between points of view.
■ Express your ideas **impersonally.** That is, using the format, 'it seems' rather than 'I think'.
■ **Compare** media texts using points, evidence and comment.
■ **Show how language is employed** in media texts.
■ Make **detailed and sustained points** on the **effectiveness of layout** in texts.
■ **Analyse (unravel) points** as well as make them.

Possible tasks include:

■ a comparison of a news event from different media
■ an analysis of a magazine or TV advert
■ the close analysis of a scene from a film or film poster
■ promotion material for a pop music CD, including its press release
■ a comparison of two soaps from different countries
■ a written account of how you planned and made a film.

GRADE BOOSTER
Anything from books to films can be called 'texts'. Use the term to get higher grades!

Question Bank 24

1 Fill the gaps in these sentences.

   a The two main skills assessed in the media assignment are

   .... and writing.

   b When you write about a media text you will be expected to analyse, review

   and ....

2 When you write about texts impersonally what pronoun must you avoid using?

   ....

3 True or false?

   a You do not need to give detailed points or ideas on texts. ....

   b To analyse means to unravel. ....

   c The media assignment tests speaking skills. ....

   d You should follow this method when writing about texts: point,

   evidence and comment. ....

   e You need to make detailed and sustained points in essays. ....

   f *Coronation Street* can be a media text. ....

   g The word 'text' can only be applied to sending messages

   on mobile phones. ....

Newspaper Terms – Checklist 1

These terms will prove useful if your teacher sets you a newspaper or magazine assignment. You may need to know the terms for your final exams as well. Let's start by going through a select list.

Newspaper terms:

- **caption** – this helps explain a picture

- **column** – newspaper articles are usually set out in several columns

- **copy** – the text of an article

- **diary column** – a gossip article or personal diary

- **editorial** – an article (column) expressing the newspaper's view on a subject

- **feature** – a particular news story with more background information from a wider range of sources (the writer's opinion will be more evident too)

- **hard news** – factual news story with little comment or analysis. Such stories answer questions of who, what, when, where and why.

- **human interest story** – a story that focuses on an individual's life: their success, endurance or failure. It might be about an unknown or famous person.

- **lead** – the main story on the front page

- **punch line** – the story's main point

- **soft news** – light news that is entertaining, colourful, less important and includes more comment.

GRADE BOOSTER

The appropriate use of correct terms in assignments or exams will lift your work and make it stand out from the crowd.

Question Bank 25

1 Where would a reader expect to see a caption?

....

2 What is a lead story?

....

3 Whose opinion is expressed in an editorial?

....

4 Fill in the gaps.

   a The main point of a story is called the ....

   b Hard news is factual news and deals with the journalist's main questions
     of: ....

   c A distinct story that has a wide range of sources and includes more
     background information and opinion is called a ....

5 Apart from a possible coursework assignment, where else might you be
expected to use newspaper or magazine terms?

....

Newspaper Terms – Checklist 2

*Here are a few more terms to impress examiners and earn you the grade that you're looking for. Remember that you can apply these terms to magazines too. **Layout** and **presentation** affect the look and design of a newspaper or magazine.*

Useful terms for layout and presentation:

- **artwork** – includes all illustrations, cartoons, maps, graphs, etc.

- **banner** – the front-page headline found at the top of the page

- **broadsheet** – refers to the larger newspapers such as *The Times, Guardian, Independent* and *Telegraph*. These papers are also known as **'the quality press'** for their in-depth reporting.

- **centre spread** – text and pictures which span across the middle pages of the newspaper

- **classified ads** – these are small advertisements grouped under subject headings and are usually not illustrated

- **colour** – some sections of newspapers, particularly the finance or business sections, are printed on coloured paper. Certain pages of a newspaper may have colour photographs. Colour can also highlight a journalist's views or simply add to impressions and descriptions of events.

- **crop** – to cut a picture down (part of the image is cut out, rather than simply making the whole image smaller).

- **display ads** – large advertisements with illustrations that sometimes appear on editorial pages

- **masthead** – the title of the newspaper at the top of a page

- **tabloids** – smaller-sized papers such as the *Daily Mail, The Sun* and *The Mirror* that specialise in sensational news and use more accessible language.

GRADE BOOSTER

It'll help you remember these terms if you look out for some of these features the next time you read a magazine or pick up a newspaper.

Question Bank 26

True or false?

1 Tabloids are larger than broadsheets. ....

2 Broadsheets have longer sentences and more in-depth
   reporting than tabloids. ....

3 Classified ads have illustrations. ....

4 To cut out part of a picture is to 'crop' it. ....

5 A centre spread is a picture across pages
   two and three of a paper. ....

6 The masthead is only found on ships. ....

7 Display ads often have illustrations. ....

8 'Artwork' is a term for any kind of illustration
   used in newspapers or magazines. ....

9 Tabloids specialise in sensational news. ....

10 Colour is used to differentiate sections of newspapers
   and magazines. Colour can also be used to add
   impressions and emphasise description. ....

Advertising to Inform and Persuade 1

*This page will help you understand a common area of difficulty with media texts: when you are asked to **analyse, review** and **comment** on **leaflets, pamphlets, flyers** and **articles**.*

The media includes direct mail advertising (also known as 'junk mail')..Analysing this can be excellent for improving your **persuasive skills** as well as **writing to inform and advise**.

Language techniques to inform or persuade

- **Alliteration**: the repetition of **consonants** is used for emphasis. It is often seen in headlines, adverts and flyers (one-sheet leaflets), along with **exaggeration**. It makes products and sales sound more exciting. For example, 'John Lewis's **S**tupendous **S**ale **S**tarts **S**aturday!'

- **Assonance** in slogans: the repetition of **vowel sounds** is useful for emphasis – for example, 'B**ea**nz m**ea**nz Heinz!'

- **Slogans** are well-known **catch phrases** that are associated with products like the one above or with popular TV programmes – for example, 'You are the weakest link – goodbye!'

- **Emotive language**: the intention is for readers to feel a specific emotion of sympathy, joy, fear, solidarity, etc. For example, 'For homeless people a star-filled sky can be deadly'.

- **Interviews and personal testimonies**: there's nothing more effective than citing a specific person. Adverts for a product might include personal recommendations from consumers – '… "It has changed my life!" Mrs Jenkins, North Wales'. A charity knows that it is difficult to relate to thousands of homeless people because they become just statistics. We can, however, relate to the suffering of a family or individual. For example, 'Home for Jim was on a windswept hill amongst some brambles.'

> ### GRADE BOOSTER
> Learn and use the terms on this page to help you get high marks in your final exams.

Question Bank 27

1 Name three types of texts that make up direct mail.

....

2 What is alliteration?

....

3 Why is alliteration used in advertising?

....

4 What is assonance?

....

5 Explain what is meant by a 'slogan'.

....

6 Why do advertisers use emotive language?

....

7 Why are interviews and personal testimonies more persuasively effective than
   general accounts of a product or a charity's work?

....

8 Apart from a possible media coursework assignment, when is the other time
   that you may be expected to use your knowledge of these techniques?

....

Advertising to Inform and Persuade 2

To complete this topic, here are a few more tips on persuasive language that can help you with difficult exam questions on leaflets, pamphlets, flyers and articles. **Remember that you not only have to comment on persuasive techniques in texts, you must also use these techniques when writing in assignments or exams.**

Language techniques to inform or persuade

- **Informal language** is intended to get readers 'on side' by persuading them that the advertisers are their friends. Advertisers are, however, wary of going too far, and keep things to the second person, 'You' or 'Dear Homeowner', etc., rather than 'Mate' or 'Love'.

- **Lists of facts** are often used to support arguments and claims. They can help readers understand issues.

- **Questions** involve readers by drawing them into claims, emotive issues, etc. For example, 'How would you feel if this was your child?' **Rhetorical questions** are used to persuade a reader rather than actually needing a reply. For example, 'How can you let this opportunity to make great savings pass you by?'

- **Repetition** of words and phrases helps make points memorable. Facts or messages are often repeated – '£10.00 a month could save a life like Jim's.'

- The **Rule of Three** is another repetitive, persuasive device. Politicians often use groups of three words or ideas in a sentence for emphasis – for example, 'This proposal is costly, dangerous and ill-advised'. Writers may begin each point with 'First', 'Second' and 'Third'.

GRADE BOOSTER

This is a crucial bank of terms to learn because good skills in persuasive language and layout could make the difference between a D and a C or much higher.

Question Bank 28

1 Informal language is:

   a Standard English ☐

   b casual language ☐

   c great for essays and assignments ☐

2 The second person is:

   a he/she ☐

   b I ☐

   c you ☐

3 Lists of facts can:

   a support a pleader's case ☐

   b drive readers to despair ☐

   c make no difference at all ☐

4 Questions can:

   a confuse readers ☐

   b draw readers in to your points and ideas ☐

   c draw readers away from points and ideas ☐

5 Repetition is used to:

   a help make points and ideas memorable ☐

   b irritate readers ☐

   c fill in gaps because there is little else to say ☐

Layout to Persuade or Inform 1

> *Presentation or layout is important because a few well-made comments in a coursework assignment or an exam will boost your marks.* **Layout is how words and pictures are presented on a page.**

Look carefully at texts that **persuade or inform** for the following features.

- **Bullet points** (like this one) help organise information into chunks and make it accessible.

- **Boxes** also make information accessible by grouping it together.

- **Graphs, diagrams and maps** make difficult information easier to grasp. Maps help customers and tourists find sales outlets and tourist attractions.

- **Headings and headlines** are used to organise information into sections for easy understanding.

- **Fonts and colours** are usually carefully chosen to suggest subtle marketing messages and ideas for products. For example, the font used for the title of the breakfast cereal *Weetabix* is carefully selected to emphasise the wholesome origins of the product.

- *Italics*, **bold** and <u>underlining</u> emphasise key points and important pieces of information for readers.

GRADE BOOSTER

Improve your skills by looking at the design of breakfast cereal and washing powder packets as well as any interesting pieces of junk mail.

Question Bank 29

True or false?

1 Bullet points help make information easier to understand.

....

2 Graphs, diagrams and maps are only put into leaflets for interest and colour.

....

3 Boxed information is easier to grasp.

....

4 Fonts and colours can suggest messages and ideas about products.

....

5 Italics and underlining can emphasise key points in persuasive and
informative texts.

....

6 Layout can help writers inform and persuade.

....

7 How layout affects persuasive texts is unimportant for the final exams.

....

Layout to Persuade or Inform 2

After you've read this page you'll be on top of this topic. Just remember to put your new knowledge into practice!

Try to identify the following features in texts that persuade or inform.

- **Logos or symbols** help identify brand names, companies and organisations such as charities. They can send out strong messages and ideas to inspire trust.

- **Catchy paragraph headings** can sum up important information such as persuasive arguments and help you understand a page without having to read all of it. They can also mark out sections of a persuasive argument so that the main argument can be easily understood.

- **Pictures and images** – appropriate pictures and images help readers understand texts and find meaning in them. Charity leaflets often feature specific images of people and show you **who** your money can help. Pictures also break up forbidding blocks of text.

- **Captions** help readers understand images and encourage a particular interpretation of them.

- **Colour in pictures and text** can carry deep meanings and associations for readers. For example, red can **symbolise** warmth, love and danger. Blue is a cold colour; it can also symbolise, for example, 'mountain freshness' and cleaning power on packets of soap powder. Colours help reinforce the advertiser's message.

GRADE BOOSTER

Remember that everything on a packet or leaflet, etc. has a purpose. Advertisers try to reach into our subconscious to persuade us.

Question Bank 30

1   Why do organisations use logos and symbols?

    ....

2   Give one purpose of catchy paragraph headings.

    ....

3   Give two reasons for including pictures in texts.

    ....

4   What are captions and how can they be used?

    ....

5   Explain how colour can add meaning to texts.

    ....

6   What is the main aim of organisations who send us leaflets and carefully
    package their products?

    ....

    ....

Subjects in Printed Advertisements 1

*If your teacher asks you to analyse an advert from a newspaper or a glossy magazine, these pages will help you make an excellent job of it. Let's start by looking at **subjects** and **audience**.*

The **subject** of an advertisement is its **product**.

Who is the target audience?

Think about the audience that the advertiser is trying to persuade. Consider the audience's age-range, sex, class and life-style. The **target audience** will determine how an advert is **set out** and **where it appears**.

Models or objects in advertisements

- Look closely at **how a product is presented**. What **status** is it linked to, including any models associated with it? Is it trying to evoke a particular **lifestyle**?

- Identify **details** such as a model's age, dress and hair style. Consider also any body language such as eye contact, facial expressions, poses or activity, etc.

- Think about the **context** of the advert. Is the advert set in another country or culture and does this add anything to the advertiser's message?

- Is the advert set in the **present, future** or **past**?

- Does the advert **conform to a particular genre**, such as romance, mystery, science fiction, etc?

- Look carefully at any **unusual objects** in the foreground or background and try to establish their **purpose**. There is a **reason** for everything.

GRADE BOOSTER

Don't suffer in silence. If you're unsure of anything in your assignment, ask your teacher to explain it further. That's their job!

Question Bank 31

1 What is the main purpose of any advertiser selling a product?

   a to persuade ☐

   b to amuse ☐

   c to entertain ☐

2 What is the second key factor for the advertiser to consider?

   a how the advert will look ☐

   b the target audience ☐

   c booking models for the advert ☐

3 Which of the following is a key feature of an advertisement's presentation?

   a facial expressions on models ☐

   b the advertiser's budget ☐

   c the magazine's cover price ☐

4 The context of an advert is its:

   a setting ☐

   b product ☐

   c price ☐

5 Objects in the foreground or background usually

   a have no significance ☐

   b have significance and a purpose ☐

   c end up in adverts by accident ☐

Subjects in Printed Advertisements 2

> *Lighting is a hidden aspect of advertisements that passes most students by. Read this page, and you'll remember to consider lighting when you analyse an advert.* ***Lighting creates mood and atmosphere.***

What is the lighting like?

Look at the lighting in the picture below. Where are the shadows? What does the lighting suggest about the scene?

There are three types of lighting: **a key light, back light** and **filler light**.

1 The **key light** is usually the brightest and most influential.

2 The **back light** helps counter glare from the key light; this makes figures appear more 'rounded'.

3 The **filler light** helps soften any shadows created by the use of the back and key lights. There may be more than one filler light.

Lighting **sets the tone** of adverts and can also help create **mood and atmosphere.** For example, lighting can create an atmosphere of mystery, romance, fantasy, etc.

The advice on lighting on this page can also be applied to the study of lighting in movies.

back light

filler light

key light

Question Bank 32

1 Lighting can create mood and .... in advertisements.

2 There are three types of lighting used in adverts: key lights, back lights and

....

3 The brightest and most influential light is the .... light.

4 The .... light helps counteract glare from the key light so that

figures and models appear more 'rounded'.

5 .... lights help soften any shadows cast by key and

back lights.

6 There can be more than one .... light.

7 Carefully chosen lighting can set the .... of an advert and

complement the advertisement's setting and genre.

Design and Layout of Advertisements

Layout is an important and often overlooked area when commenting on the persuasiveness of adverts. There's really nothing to it because it all comes down to this: **layout is about how space is used**.

Ask the following questions of an advertisement's layout.

Colour

- How is colour used in the advert?
- What colour is the background?
- What is the symbolic significance or message given by the use of colours in the advert?

Fonts and type size

- What are the fonts like? Which parts of the text are in larger or smaller type size?
- What messages or impressions are suggested by the selected fonts?

Graphic devices

- Do graphs or charts appear in the advert?
- Explain why you think they are there.

Space

- How is space used within the advert?
- Does an image fill much of the available space? If so, why?
- What does empty space suggest in your advert?

> ### GRADE BOOSTER
> You'll get the top grades as long as you remember to do the following when writing essays: make a *point*, give *evidence* and *comment* on your evidence.

Question Bank 33

1 What is layout all about?

....

2 Identify four important aspects of layout to examine.

....

3 Give one purpose for the use of colour in adverts.

....

4 Why might an advertiser favour one font more than another?

....

5 What are 'graphic devices'?

....

6 How might an advertiser use the space around their product?

....

7 What method should you use in arguments in essays to get maximum marks?

....

Persuasive Techniques in Advertisements

This page will not help just with printed advertisements, it will make short work of TV commercials too. Let's examine the persuasive methods of advertisers.

Persuasive techniques are methods of persuasion.

Examine the advertisement to see if any of the following are present.

- **Promises of benefits** (advantageous promises) such as prizes, improvements in lifestyle, freedom, added sexual attractiveness, or saving money.

- **A feeling of belonging**: does buying the product identify you with a group, trend, etc?

- **Appeals to conscience**: are you being moved to feeling pity or a sense of commitment for your family, etc?

- **Celebrities or experts**: does the advert use people associated with the product or people known from other fields?

- **Witnesses or personal testimony**: are you being told that the product worked for 'Mr Jones'? What is gained by using ordinary people?

- **Figures of speech**: does the advert rely for its message on puns, personification, alliteration, etc?

- **Dazzled by jargon**: is the advertiser trying to impress you with unusual words or phrases?

- **Genre and conventions**: does the genre of the advert match the expected conventions of that genre? For instance, is the representation of an office realistic or dreamlike?

- **Hard information**: is there a reliance on statistics, facts, figures, etc?

- **Rule of three**: what messages or words are grouped in threes?

GRADE BOOSTER

There's no need to say everything when writing essays. Arguing a few points well is better than making many points badly!

Question Bank 34

1 Which of the following is an 'advantageous promise'?

   a Buy one and get one free!

   b Mr Jones says that he will buy our product again.

   c It does exactly what it says on the tin.

2 An 'appeal to conscience' is

   a intended to save your money and make you forget the product

   b intended to move you to pity or duty to your family, etc.

   c the last resort of a scoundrel

3 Celebrities and experts appear in adverts because

   a they love fame

   b they can lend credibility to products

   c they have nothing better to do

4 Figures of speech are used in adverts because

   a they can emphasise messages about products

   b they sound good

   c they make speakers sound important

5 To be 'dazzled by jargon' means

   a you've stayed up too late at a party

   b advertisers are trying to impress you with technical
      words about products

   c an alien has landed from the planet Zorg and is
      deafening you with a speech gun

Features of TV and Radio Commercials 1

If you've been set an assignment on TV or radio commercials, this page will help with key technical terms. To begin, let's look at the storyline features of adverts.

Persuasive features of adverts

Here are some storyline features to consider.

- **Narrative and plot**: is there a storyline in the commercial? If so, how does it sell the product?

- **Genre**: what kind of story is presented? Is it a thriller, adventure, comedy, etc.? How does the genre contribute to the message?

- **Setting**: when and where is the commercial set and does it add to the persuasiveness of the message?

- **Use of stereotypes**: these are quick ways of understanding **types of people or characters**, such as policemen, busy housewives, vicars, etc., when time is short.

- **Values and ideology**: what values and beliefs seem to be present within the commercial? Look for values with which the audience is expected to agree, such as: law and order, family values, saving money, etc.

- **Target audience**: who is the commercial aimed at? This can be determined by the time of day or night it is broadcast and the programmes that it appears within and between.

GRADE BOOSTER

Try to use technical terms in assignments because teachers and examiners will reward you for doing so.

Question Bank 35

1   What is the word for the plot in a commercial?

    ....

2   What does 'genre' mean?

    ....

3   Why do advertisers use character stereotypes?

    ....

4   Give two key features of setting for TV and radio commercials.

    ....

5   Briefly explain what 'values and ideology' means.

    ....

6   What does the term 'target audience' mean?

    ....

7   When you write about the media in assignments and essays what
    must you try to include?

    ....

Features of TV and Radio Commercials 2

After you've read this page you'll feel much more confident about this topic. Many of the features below would apply to all forms of advertising.

More persuasive features

Check if these features apply to your assignment.

- **Key words as persuaders**: *free, only, health, natural, quality, smooth, value, unique,* etc.
- **'Before and after'**: spots, cleaner clothes, headaches, whiter teeth, etc.
- **'Perfect' images**: the sun is shining, everyone's happy and smiling, clothes are brighter, glasses sparkle, food looks appetising, etc.
- **Bandwagon or 'keeping up with the Joneses'**: you need what others have; the product will improve your **lifestyle** too.
- **The genuine article**: the product is its own **brand**: e.g. Levis®, Coca Cola®, Pepsi®, etc.

Using sound

- **Music** to create mood and atmosphere. Modern pop songs can make products seem youthful, trendy, etc.
- **Diagetic and non-diagetic sound**: *diagetic* sound is realistic sound that naturally occurs within a commercial. *Non-diagetic* sound is music or other sounds that have been deliberately inserted. Explain the persuasive effects of added sounds. You can use these terms to comment on films too.
- **Voiceovers**: these are often deeply reassuring male voices endorsing products. Voiceovers can also set a **mood** of excitement, etc.
- **Increased volume**: although this is usually denied by advertisers, it sometimes sounds as if the volume increases when the commercials begin.

GRADE BOOSTER

Remember to *record* your commercial so that you can replay it as many times as you need to.

Question Bank 36

True or false?

1 Key words can act as persuaders.

   ....

2 The camera never lies about products.

   ....

3 The 'before and after' technique would not suit a toothpaste commercial.

   ....

4 Advertisers sometimes identify their brands as the product.

   ....

5 'Bandwagon' means 'Get your wagons in a circle!'

   ....

6 Pop songs can create mood and identify the product with a particular
   audience.

   ....

7 Non-diagectic sound is deliberately added for persuasive effect.

   ....

8 Diagectic sound is deliberately added for persuasive effect.

   ....

Story-Telling With Cameras 1

> *The terms on this page will be useful for commenting on TV commercials,*
> *programmes or movies. Looking at film may never be the same again!*

The grammar of film: how camera shots are framed

The movie camera tells stories in a visual way. Audiences need to know **where the
action takes place, which characters are important and their feelings and
emotions**.

■ **Scenes** are the **main settings** where action/dialogue takes place (in a market
or house, etc.) A scene can last from a few seconds to several minutes.

Important kinds of shot for places and characters

■ An **establishing shot** places the scene in a **time or place**. For instance, a shot
of Big Ben informs viewers that the action takes place in London.

■ **Total** or **long shots** let audiences know **who** the significant characters are
because you can see them **from head to toe**.

■ **Mid** or **half shots** show characters' heads, chests and shoulders.

■ **Close-ups** can be of characters' faces or even parts of their faces or hands
(**extreme close ups**). They can show all kinds of emotions.

■ **Point of view shots** show what a character can see; the camera takes the
place of a character. These shots are used to give a documentary feel in
scenes.

Question Bank 37

1 A scene is a .... where the action takes place for a few

seconds or longer.

2 An .... shot tells the audience where a scene is taking place.

3 Characters' heads, chests and shoulders are shown in ....

shots.

4 Camera shots that show just the head or parts of the body are known as

....

5 When you can see the whole of a character's body this is known as a

.... shot.

6 .... can show a range of emotions from joy to fear.

7 When the camera shows us what a character sees this is known as a

.... shot.

Story-Telling With Cameras 2

Here are a few more terms to consider when studying film. Once you've completed this page you'll know how to write an excellent assignment!

More shots that help tell stories

In television, directors often prefer that no more than two characters be in a room at the same time. If there are more than two, the camera tends to focus on just two characters speaking at a time.

Examine your TV programme or film for these shots and their effects.

- **High-angle shots** look down on characters and tend to make them appear **vulnerable**.

- **Low-angle shots** look up at characters and often make them seem **powerful**. Both types of shot can be used as point of view shots.

- **Tracking or dolly shot**: the camera moves from one place to another.

- **Cut**: signifies a change of **scene** or **time**.

- **Dissolve** is a technique where one scene seems to dissolve into another to show **time passing**.

- **Montage** is **rapid editing** that creates an impression from a wide variety of shots.

- **Zoom**: the camera focuses in on a subject, so we can no longer see the background. When the camera quickly zooms in on a character, it can depict shock, surprise, etc.

- **Wipe**: one scene *wipes* another from the frame.

GRADE BOOSTER

A particularly impressive term is *mise en scène*. It refers to everything that you can see in a frame, particularly the setting. It's a good one to use when discussing stills from films.

Question Bank 38

1 What two things can a cut signify?

....

2 How does a high-angle shot make characters appear?

....

3 What is the effect of low-angle shots on characters?

....

4 What is montage?

....

5 Explain what *mise en scène* means.

....

6 What happens when a director uses 'wipe'?

....

7 What is a tracking or dolly shot?

....

8 How many speaking characters are ideal for scenes in rooms?

....

Shakespeare Grading Criteria

Lots of students find Shakespeare difficult. We'll make sure that you're not one of them by giving you the help that you need over the next few pages.

The main skills examined in the Shakespeare section are **reading and understanding**.

Look carefully at the marking criteria to help you achieve a top grade.

For a C you will need to show **insight** when you write about:

- **characters, stagecraft and structure**
- **use of language**
- the **main ideas** in the play as well as their **relevance** and **implications** for Shakespeare's time.

For a B you will need to show **analytical skills** when discussing:

- **characters, stagecraft and structure**
- the play's **relevance** for people in **Shakespeare's time** and **implications** of **historical issues**
- Shakespeare's **language** and especially his **imagery.**

For an A you will need to show **interpretive and analytical skills** when considering:

- the play's **moral, historical and philosophical context**
- how the play sits within its **genre**
- Shakespeare's **use of language for dramatic, poetic and figurative effect**.

For an A* you will need to show **originality of analysis** and **flair in interpretation** when evaluating:

- the play's **moral, historical and philosophical** significance
- Shakespeare's **stagecraft and appeal** for his audience
- **patterns and details** of words and images.

GRADE BOOSTER

If this sounds frightening, don't worry. Apart from the *historical context* you'll probably only have to meet *some* of the criteria from any section.

Question Bank 39

True or false?

1 To get a C you will have to mention some of your play's main ideas and state their relevance and implications for people when Shakespeare wrote his play.

   ....

2 You can get by in an essay on Shakespeare without referring in detail to his use of language.

   ....

3 You may be asked to discuss Shakespeare's stagecraft (the art of writing and staging plays) in your assignment.

   ....

4 To get an A you may need to comment on how the play sits within its genre.

   ....

5 To achieve an A* you may be expected to make sustained comments on patterns and details of Shakespeare's language and imagery.

   ....

6 Interpretive and analytical skills are hardly used when studying Shakespeare.

   ....

7 The main skills examined in Shakespeare assignments are reading and understanding.

   ....

Shakespeare's Language: Poetic Verse

> To understand Shakespeare you'll need to understand how he uses **three styles of language**. Let's begin by looking at how Shakespeare uses **poetic verse**. Poetic verse is **rhymed verse**.

Shakespeare's three styles of language are employed in some of the greatest plots ever written. He used poetic verse, blank verse and prose.

Poetic verse

Poetic verse (rhymed lines) can **signify the end of scenes and acts**. After discussing a possible marriage for Juliet, the Capulets are informed of the arrival of the first guests to a family party intended to introduce Juliet to County Paris:

Lady Capulet:	We follow thee; Juliet the County <u>stays.</u>
Nurse:	Go, girl, seek happy nights to happy <u>days</u>.

Shakespeare also uses **poetic verse for dramatic effect**; for example, when love-struck Romeo first sees Juliet he touches her hand as if she is a saint. He maintains the pilgrimage metaphor as he begins a love sonnet asking Juliet to grant him a kiss:

Romeo:	If I profane with my unworthiest <u>hand</u>
	This holy shrine, the gentle sin is <u>this:</u>
	My lips, two blushing pilgrims, ready <u>stand</u>
	To smooth that rough touch with a tender <u>kiss.</u>

(Romeo and Juliet Act 1, Scene 5)

Find and read the next ten lines of this **sonnet** and consider its emotional impact. What is gained from writing the couple's first meeting in **poetic verse**?

GRADE BOOSTER

Remember that Shakespeare *matches* his *style of language* to characters' thoughts, feelings and circumstances.

Question Bank 40

1 Shakespeare used .... styles of language in his plays.

2 Poetic verse is .... verse.

3 .... verse is employed as a device by Shakespeare to mark the ends of scenes and acts.

4 The other two styles of writing are .... and prose.

5 Shakespeare also uses poetic verse for .... effect.

6 Shakespeare always matches his style of .... to characters' thoughts, feelings, and circumstances.

7 In prologues and moments of high drama, Shakespeare sometimes inserts .... into his plays.

Shakespeare's Language: Blank Verse

> *Shakespeare uses blank verse and prose much more often than poetic verse in his plays. Let's think about how he uses **blank verse**. Blank verse is **unrhymed verse**.*

Blank verse is metrical, elevated speech, intended by Shakespeare to represent **the rhythms of everyday speech**. Noble characters use it to emphasise their status or emotions:

Romeo: *But soft, what light through yonder window breaks?*

(Romeo and Juliet Act 2, Scene 2)

Shakespeare's **form** for blank verse is **iambic pentameter**. This means that his rhythm is expressed through **stressed and unstressed syllables in lines of five feet**.

An **iamb** is a kind of *foot*. Put simply, there are roughly **ten syllables** on each line. We say 'roughly' because Shakespeare sometimes varies the number from nine to eleven on each line. It evens out to ten in the end!

To sum up, there are **two syllables in one iamb**. There are **five iambs in a line of iambic pentameter**.

Shakespeare's line of five feet looks like this, with the stressed syllables shown in bold:

Romeo: *But **soft**,/ what **light**/ through **yon**/der **win**/dow **breaks**?*

Read the sentence aloud to hear the rhythm for yourself.

Trochees

Sometimes Shakespeare **reverses the expected rhythm of his iambs** to express a deeply emotional state in a character. When Romeo thinks that Juliet is dead he drinks a poisonous potion as a final toast to his Juliet:

Romeo: ***Here's** to my **love**!* (He drinks.) *O **true** a/**poth**/e/**car**/y.*

In the first foot of this line, the first syllable, *Here's*, is stressed. This kind of rhythm (foot) is known as a *trochee*. In a trochee, **the first syllable is stressed and the second unstressed**. Notice how its reversed rhythm emphasises Romeo's despair.

GRADE BOOSTER

Don't despair if you've found this page difficult! Sometimes understanding takes time. Come back to it again if you need to.

Question Bank 41

1. What is blank verse? ....

2. Who might be expected to speak it? ....

3. What rhythms does Shakespeare wish to imitate through his
   use of blank verse? ....

4. Give the name for the form of blank verse used in Shakespeare's time.

   ....

5. How many feet are there in a line of blank verse? ....

6. An iamb has two syllables in it. How many feet does each iamb take up in a
   line of iambic pentameter?

   ....

7. How is each syllable stressed in an iamb?

   ....

8. What can the inclusion of a trochee do to iambic rhythm?

   ....

9. Why does Shakespeare sometimes like to reverse his rhythm in blank verse?

   ....

10. Which is more commonly found in Shakespeare's plays: poetic verse or
    blank verse?

    ....

Shakespeare's Language: Prose

> *Prose is the easiest style of language used by Shakespeare for us to understand, because it's closest to the language that we use today.*
> ***Prose is ordinary speech.***

How Shakespeare uses prose

Prose is ordinary language spoken by characters of any status. Shakespeare mainly uses prose with uneducated characters such as servants or clowns. It is **speech that lacks dramatic intensity**.

Prose is employed in witty exchanges and comic interludes and serves to advance Shakespeare's plots. Take, for example, this exchange between the servants of the Capulets and Montagues in the beginning of *Romeo and Juliet*. An insult that leads to an all-out street battle:

Gregory: *I will frown as I pass by, and let them take it as they list.*

Sampson: *Nay, as they dare. I will bite my thumb at them, which is disgrace to them, if they bear it.*

Abr: *Do you bite your thumb at us, sir?*

Sampson: *I do bite my thumb, sir.*

When servants and uneducated characters try to imitate their masters' behaviour or speech the result can be comic and sometimes tragic.

> ### GRADE BOOSTER
> If you can work out the type of language a character is using, you're half way to understanding Shakespeare's use of language.

Question Bank 42

1 Why does Shakespeare use prose?

   a because it rhymes ☐

   b because it sounds like blank verse ☐

   c because it sounds like ordinary speech ☐

2 Which characters is prose used for?

   a characters of any status ☐

   b characters of high status ☐

   c characters who are servants or clowns ☐

3 Prose is language which:

   a has dramatic intensity ☐

   b lacks dramatic intensity ☐

   c Shakespeare uses all the time ☐

4 Prose helps Shakespeare to:

   a develop his plots ☐

   b bore the pants off his audience ☐

   c describe characters' emotions ☐

5 Who is most likely to use prose?

   a characters of high rank ☐

   b characters of low rank ☐

   c characters who can't think up rhymes ☐

Shakespeare's Imagery

> *Once you've understood Shakespeare's choice of language, his imagery shouldn't be a problem.* **Imagery means figures of speech or word pictures.**

Shakespeare invests his language with **imagery** for these reasons:

- To make points in dialogue and action.
- To draw attention to themes and ideas.
- To develop characters and plots.

In order to do these things he uses:

- **Similes** – comparisons using 'as' or 'like'. For instance, 'The girl is like a flower'.

- **Metaphors** – stronger comparisons in which one thing is said to *be* something else using 'is' or 'are' or through implying it. For instance, 'The girl is a flower'.

- **Personification** (person-making) – a stronger metaphor in which animals or inanimate objects are given human characteristics. When Lord Capulet thinks that Juliet is dead he says:

  Death is my heir;
  My daughter he hath wedded.

- **Motifs** – ideas, characters, images or themes that recur within texts. For instance, death is mentioned several times and becomes a motif in *Romeo and Juliet*. In the Prologue the tragic destiny of the lovers is emphasised early with:

  The fearful passage of their death-mark'd love.

- **Oxymorons** – contradictory words and phrases juxtaposed (put next to each other) for dramatic effect. They can be used to show emotional turmoil and other effects in characters. For example, Juliet is briefly bewildered after hearing from the Nurse that Romeo has killed her cousin, Tybalt:

  A damned saint, an honourable villain!

GRADE BOOSTER

Look for examples of imagery in your play. It'll do wonders for your writing skills and grades!

Question Bank 43

True or false?

1 The term 'imagery' means figures of speech or word pictures. ....

2 The main reason Shakespeare uses imagery is because
   he likes to decorate his plays. ....

3 A metaphor is a comparison using 'as' or 'like'. ....

4 A simile is a comparison using 'as' or 'like'. ....

5 'Personification' means that characters impersonate each other. ....

6 The following are oxymorons: *alone together, pretty ugly, terribly pleased,
   definitely maybe, found missing, almost exactly* and *living dead.* ....

7 Shakespeare uses oxymorons to emphasise confused states in characters or
   unusual happenings. ....

8 A motif is something Shakespearean characters wear on their costumes.

   ....

9 Knowledge of how Shakespeare uses imagery will improve your grades.

   ....

10 Personification is a powerful metaphor. ....

Shakespeare's Characters

> *Now you have studied Shakespeare's language, you need to figure out his characters. Study these pages and you'll find that Shakespeare's characters are easy to understand.*

How to study Shakespeare's characters

As you read your play look for some of the points given below to help you find out about characters.

- **The audience's impressions of and sympathy with characters**. These can change!

- **What they say** – look for speeches in which they give themselves away while expressing innermost thoughts in **dramatic monologues**. That is, while **speaking alone.** Shakespeare used the device so that audiences could overhear characters' thoughts.

- **What they do and how they behave** – examine how characters do things (cautiously? impulsively? bravely? etc.) Why?

- **What other characters say about them** – much can be gleaned from what other characters say about your chosen character. This also includes any **imagery** such as **comparisons** with birds or animals.

- **What stage directions reveal about their traits of behaviour.** Shakespeare gives few stage directions. However, brief two-word directions can show characters' impulsiveness, caution, etc.

- **How they change and develop in the scene, act or play.** Romeo changes from a self-pitying juvenile into a man and heroic lover.

- **How and why they cannot change.** Tybalt Capulet, another passionate youth in *Romeo and Juliet,* cannot overcome his desire for vengeance on the Montagues. Similar characters in Shakespeare either die or are punished.

GRADE BOOSTER

Make useful notes on important characters by writing a profile for each one, using the headings above.

Question Bank 44

1   What is the dramatic term for a character speaking alone?

    ....

2   What does this device help an audience to understand?

    ....

3   You can learn about characters from what they .... and how
    they behave.

4   Notice how characters .... and develop in plays.

5   Characters who cannot .... can also be significant in
    Shakespeare's plays. However such characters are usually punished in one
    way or another.

6   Brief stage .... can also act as an indicator to character traits.

7   Good notes on characters can be produced by writing ....
    on them.

Shakespeare's Characters: Romeo

> *Here's a brief profile of Romeo, the tragic hero from 'Romeo and Juliet'.*
> *After you've read this page why not write a few character profiles from your play?*

Romeo is a complex character who becomes a true tragic hero through the power of his love for Juliet.

Audience's impressions

At first these are not very good. He wallows in exaggerated self-pity after being rejected by Rosaline:

> *She hath forsworn to love, and in that vow*
> *Do I live dead that live to tell it now.*

However, when Romeo first meets Juliet this aspect of his character fades as he expresses his passionate love for her through a great sonnet. (See Act 1, Scene 5.)

Other characters' views

Romeo's friends and enemies tell us that the Romeo of the beginning of the play is not the real Romeo. His family's bitter enemy, Lord Capulet, is an excellent witness for Romeo's true character for, as he tells an angry Tybalt:

> *And to say the truth, Verona brags of him*
> *To be a virtuous and well govern'd youth.*

After a playful battle of wits, Romeo's friend, Mercutio, welcomes back the friend he knew:

> *Now art thou sociable, now art thou Romeo.*

Romeo's actions

Romeo is young, passionate, impulsive and sometimes immature. He rushes into everything: love, marriage and even suicide. The audience's reaction is usually, 'If only he'd waited a little longer before drinking the poison!'

GRADE BOOSTER
Don't try to cover everything in profiles. A few good points will do.

Question Bank 45

1 Early in *Romeo and Juliet* the audience are unlikely to sympathise
   with Romeo because:

   a he wallows in self-pity ☐

   b he is a teenager ☐

   c he is a hit with Rosaline ☐

2 By the time Romeo meets Juliet the audience change their minds about him
   because:

   a he is only a youth ☐

   b he is capable of great passion and love when he falls for Juliet ☐

   c he is still feeling sorry for himself ☐

3 Other characters, like Lord Capulet:

   a speak well of Romeo ☐

   b disparage Romeo ☐

   c say little of Romeo ☐

4 Once Romeo falls in love with Juliet he returns to being:

   a a sociable and fun-loving character ☐

   b a sad loner ☐

   c a party pooper ☐

5 Romeo's actions in the play show him to be:

   a cautious and wise ☐

   b impulsive ☐

   c inactive ☐

Shakespeare's Plots and Structure

*This page will enable you to understand a typical **plot** of a Shakespeare play. What follows should be helpful even if it is a little bit oversimplified.*
***A plot is the** outline of a play; it is what happens.*

Look for this kind of structure in your play:

- In the first act the **main characters are introduced** and their strengths and weaknesses exposed. The world is in **natural harmony** and order and authority are respected.

- **In Acts 2–3 problems begin to occur.** Order is undermined as authority is undermined and things begin to go wrong. All kinds of jokes, deceptions and murders begin to occur.

- **Acts 4–5 usually see things reach a climax.** If you are reading a **tragedy** then central characters such as Romeo and Juliet or Macbeth die. The play now reaches its highest moment of **dramatic intensity**.

- **The aftermath sees order and the proper authority in control once more.** Society is at one with nature, new kings are crowned, couples get married and lessons are learned.

Shakespeare's plots probably owe a great deal to the insecurity that people felt at the time about the ageing and childless Queen Elizabeth. The lack of an heir was likely to lead to instability and conflict. It was the son of Elizabeth's executed rival, Mary Queen of Scots, who became James I in 1603.

GRADE BOOSTER

Notice how Shakespeare makes *dramatic contrasts* within his plays by placing a comic scene before a serious one and vice versa. One result is that moments of high drama become more intense.

Question Bank 46

1 In which parts of a Shakespeare play will harmony and order prevail?

....

2 When do the problems and complications really get going?

....

3 What is the highest point of drama in the play called?

....

4 What can happen during the climax of a play?

....

5 Briefly explain what tends to happen at the end of Shakespeare's plays.

....

6 How could the structure of many of Shakespeare's plays be said to reflect the concerns of the early audiences who watched them?

....

7 Explain how Shakespeare uses contrasts in scenes to make moments of high drama stand out more.

....

Categories of Shakespeare's Plays

When reading a Shakespeare play you need to establish whether it's a **history** *play, a* **tragedy** *or a* **comedy**. *Once the* **genre** *is known it may help you when studying the play's plot and themes.*

There are three kinds of Shakespeare plays: tragedies, histories and comedies.

Some plays in the comedies category can also be known as *tragi-comedies*. A prime example of this is *Romeo and Juliet.* What is the category of the play that you are studying?

Shakespeare did not specify these categories. They first appeared seven years after Shakespeare's death in the first Folio edition of the plays published in 1623.

Here are some of **the mostly likely plays** that you'll study at GCSE and their **possible** categories:

History Plays (mostly about kingship)	Tragedies	Comedies
Henry IV, Part 1	*Antony and Cleopatra*	*All's Well That Ends Well*
Henry IV, Part 2	*Julius Caesar*	*As You Like It*
Henry V	*Macbeth*	*The Comedy of Errors*
Richard II	*Othello*	*Love's Labour's Lost*
Richard III	*Romeo and Juliet*	*Measure For Measure*
		The Merchant Of Venice
		A Midsummer-Night's Dream
		Much Ado About Nothing
		The Taming Of The Shrew
		The Tempest
		Twelfth Night

Some of the plays overlap into other categories. So it's best not to be too rigid in categorising them.

> ### GRADE BOOSTER
>
> **If you can, go to see a live performance of your play. Shakespeare intended his plays to be performed, not read. Live performances also make the language easier to understand and the story more memorable.**

Question Bank 47

1 How many kinds of play did Shakespeare write?

   a two ☐

   b three ☐

   c one ☐

2 Some people claim that there is a fourth type of play. What is this category?

   a comedy romance ☐

   b musical romance ☐

   c tragi-comedy ☐

3 How many years after Shakespeare's death were the categories first made?

   a 25 ☐

   b 7 ☐

   c 200 ☐

4 Which of the following is a history play?

   a *Romeo and Juliet* ☐

   b *Henry IV, Part 1* ☐

   c *Othello* ☐

5 Which of the following is a comedy?

   a *Macbeth* ☐

   b *Richard III* ☐

   c *Much Ado About Nothing* ☐

6 The best way to understand Shakespeare is:

   a to see a performance ☐

   b to read the text ☐

   c to ask your best friend ☐

Ideas and Themes in Shakespeare 1

> *It's amazing how the **same themes and ideas** keep cropping up in Shakespeare's plays. Check to see if any of the four themes below are in your play. **Themes are the main messages and ideas.***

The following themes and messages are found in several plays:

■ **Contrast between appearance and reality** is found in most **tragedies and comedies**. This theme may reflect economic changes in Shakespeare's time when puritans and thrifty yeoman farmers gained more power and influence at the expense of the nobility (who seemed more powerful).

■ **Change** affects characters in every play. **Some characters change and develop; other characters cannot change.** Proud Benedict and Beatrice from *Much Ado About Nothing* think that they will 'never marry' yet they are quite happy to marry each other by the end of the play. From the same play, Don John, Don Pedro's 'bastard half brother', hates and envies his brother for his title and lands; he briefly revenges himself on Don Pedro by undermining Don Pedro's friends. Don John is eventually caught and, like several Shakespearean villains, faces his punishment 'tomorrow'.

■ **Conflict, hatred and war** are present in many plays and in particular: *Julius Caesar, Romeo and Juliet, The Merchant of Venice, Henry IV, Parts 1 and 2, Henry V* and several others.

■ **Fate or fortune** (the notion that characters' lives are predetermined, sometimes by a goddess) is an important feature of many plays.

GRADE BOOSTER

Think about how these themes apply to your play. Once you've identified the themes and ideas in your play, you're well on the way to understanding it.

Question Bank 48

1. What does the term 'theme' mean?

   ....

2. What could the theme of the contrast between appearance and reality imply about Shakespeare's time?

   ....

3. When characters change and develop in Shakespeare's plays they tend to do well. What usually happens when characters cannot change?

   ....

4. Identify two plays in which you would expect to find the themes of conflict, war or hatred?

   ....

5. The Elizabethans and Jacobeans believed in it. Many of Shakespeare's characters believe that they are victims of it. What is it?

   ....

6. Why is it useful to identify themes and ideas in a play?

   ....

Ideas and Themes in Shakespeare 2

> *Here are a few more themes to look out for in your play. Remember that themes are messages and ideas.*

Are these themes and ideas present in your play?

- **Good and evil** is often found in many plays.

- **Loyalty and love and marriage** can be found in several plays and especially comedies. Friendship is also explored in several plays.

- **Order and disorder and order again** can be found in most plays. The structure of Shakespeare's plays tends to follow this model.

- **Self-knowledge** is found in each of the three categories of plays. Characters who are incapable of acknowledging their faults, such as Malvolio in *Twelfth Night* and Shylock in *The Merchant of Venice*, are invariably punished or humbled.

- **Kingship and justice** are important themes in many plays. Shakespeare's fellow citizens wanted stability and justice above anything else. They knew that only a wise and just ruler would uphold the law and thus make society safe.

There may be other key themes in the play you are studying.

Can you think of any?

Notes on themes:

- ....

- ....

- ....

GRADE BOOSTER

Plays often have more than one theme. Think through the implications of your play's themes. What do they suggest about people's concerns in Shakespeare's time?

Question Bank 49

1 The theme of good and evil is found in:

   a every play ☐

   b many plays ☐

   c one play ☐

2 The theme of self-knowledge is present when:

   a a character changes their beliefs and behaviour
   because of what they have learned ☐

   b a character makes a scientific discovery ☐

   c a character is abducted by aliens ☐

3 The theme of love and marriage is present:

   a only in comedies ☐

   b in several plays ☐

   c only in tragedies ☐

4 Shakespeare's structure of 'order, disorder and the
re-establishment of order' can be found in:

   a two plays ☐

   b most plays ☐

   c three plays ☐

5 The theme of kingship and justice possibly reflects
that fact that the people in Shakespeare's time:

   a loved their rulers ☐

   b were worried about the transition to a new king ☐

   c hated their rulers ☐

A Shakespeare Essay Plan

> *Clear planning is the key to success. Have a look at this plan for the following question on 'Romeo and Juliet' to see what we mean.*

Essay question: *Why is the ending of Shakespeare's 'Romeo and Juliet' so tragic?'*

Essay plan

1 Introduction

2 Begin where Romeo hears Balthasar's mistaken bad news and Romeo's reactions to it. The tragedy of the couple's deaths begins to gather pace in Act Five.

3 **Discuss other tragic events**: the 'pestilence' prevents Friar Lawrence's warning letter from being delivered to Romeo; Romeo buys poison from an impoverished apothecary; the unwitting Paris fights Romeo and dies, etc.

4 **Analyse** the **saddest** and **most ironic** parts of Romeo or Juliet's final speeches and explain **why** they are tragic.

5 **Explain what is tragic in other characters' final speeches.** Who else dies and why are their deaths tragic?

6 What would **audiences in Shakespeare's day** have made of the ending? What did they think of **secret marriages**? *

   - Secret marriages and why they were socially dangerous.
   - How families like the Capulets tried to improve their status through marrying into richer or royal families.

7 What is **your response** to the tragic ending?

8 Conclusion

* (The paragraph or so on historical context can go near the beginning; however, in this essay it will have more impact towards the end.)

> ### GRADE BOOSTER
> **Never lose sight of the title of your essay. It'll help you to keep everything you write relevant.**

Question Bank 50

1 What is a key factor for success in writing essays?

    ....

2 Where do you need to put your paragraph or so on historical context?

    ....

3 If you were to use this essay plan for the question on *Romeo and Juliet,* give
   one topic on the historical context that you would need to research and then
   write about.

    ....

4 Which kind of language do you think Shakespeare chose for Romeo and
   Juliet's final speeches: blank verse or prose?

    ....

5 Why would they use this type of speech?

    ....

6 If you commented on Shakespeare's audience's reactions to themes and
   ideas within his plays, would this fulfil the criteria for giving historical context in
   your essay?

    ....

7 Should you give your own views on texts at the end of your essay and
   nowhere else?

    ....

Heritage Poets in Paper 2

> *Let's take a look at the poetry section of the exam.* **Poets in the English literary heritage are poets born within the British Isles.**

The poetry section in Paper 2 tests **reading and understanding skills** (in the NEAB exam it takes up two half-hour slots of a two-hour exam). The second hour tests **writing skills** to explain, inform or describe.

All the exam boards must test **reading and understanding skills** through a mixture of extracts from novels and stories or through poetry. SEG, for instance, has its own selections of poets or poems arranged under **specific topics or themes.**

The marks available for Poets in the English Literary Heritage and the next section from the same paper called Poems from Other Cultures and Traditions account for 15% of your GCSE.

Your teacher will select one poet's poems for study. NEAB at present offers groups of poems by Simon Armitage, Carol Ann Duffy and Ted Hughes.

Each poet's poems will have been chosen carefully for similarities in **themes and ideas.** For instance, Carol Ann Duffy writes about the experience of being 'An Outsider' in two poems and 'Different Kinds of Love' in others.

GRADE BOOSTER

The first thing to do is to understand your poems. Then try to discover common themes and ideas.

Question Bank 51

1 Poets in the English Literary Heritage were born in the ....
   Isles.

2 The poetry section in Paper 2 tests .... and
   .... skills.

3 All the exam boards test these skills by grouping short stories, extracts from
   novels and poems under specific .... and themes.

4 In the NEAB exam, the two sets of poems – English Literary Heritage and
   Poems From Other Cultures and Traditions – are worth ....% of the
   mark for English at GCSE.

5 Each set of poems is allocated .... minutes in Paper 2 by the
   exam board.

6 The selection of poems that you study from one poet will be linked by
   .... and ideas.

7 The first thing to do when reading a poem is to try to understand it. The
   second is to find .... between the poems.

Grading Criteria for Poetry

The main skills examined are **reading and understanding**.

You only have half an hour to compare two poems. Aim to make a few relevant
points well rather than lots of points badly. You also need a brief plan with the
Higher paper, as there may not be any bullet points to help you.

Answers within the C to B range are likely to have:

- a **sustained and developed response** using cross references
- **effective supportive detail** with brief, integrated quotations
- an **understanding of the form and rhythm** of the poems
- an **appreciation of concerns, attitudes and ideas** in poems
- a **personal response** to the poem's language.

Answers within the A range will also show:

- an awareness of **the poet's intentions**
- **sensitive insight** when exploring poems
- **empathy** with the poet's concerns, ideas and attitudes
- an **awareness of the poems' form and structure** and how this contributes to **themes and ideas**
- a **personal evaluation** of the poems.

Answers in the A* range will also include:

- **consistent insight** with close textual analysis
- a **convincing and imaginative interpretation** of the poems
- a **high degree of personal empathy** with the poet's intentions
- an **enthusiastic personal response**.

GRADE BOOSTER

You can't get more than a low C unless you write about *two* or
more poems!

Question Bank 52

True or false?

1 The two main skills examined in poetry are speaking and listening.

....

2 You need to make a brief essay plan for the Higher paper because there may
be no bullet points to lead you through the question.

....

3 You need effective supportive detail with brief, integrated quotations to get a
minimum of a C or B grade.

....

4 There is no need to give a personal response or an evaluation of a poem's
language and ideas to get a high grade.

....

5 A high degree of personal empathy with the poet's intentions is necessary for
an A* grade.

....

6 There is no need for close textual analysis to get a high grade for poetry.

....

7 The highest grade you can get is a low C unless you write about two or
more poems.

....

Poetry Skills: Sound

> *You'll get very high grades if you can recognise the techniques poets use to make their poems seem life-like, convincing and memorable.* **Sounds can create effects.**

Poets use sound for a variety of effects:

- **Alliteration** is the use of the same consonant at the beginning of words for emphasis. For instance, in Carol Ann Duffy's 'War Photographer' the poet emphasises how suffering and war are found across the world with:

  Belfast. Beirut. Phnom Penh. All flesh is grass.[1]

- **Assonance** is the repetition of vowel sounds. In this example from Duffy's 'Stealing' the 'mate's' coldness is emphasised by **assonance** within this **simile**:

  ... I wanted him, a mate
  with a mind as cold as the slice of ice [2]

- **Onomatopoeia** is a word that sounds like its meaning; this device can bring the **senses** into poetry: e.g. *'crash'*, *'pop'*, etc.

- **Sibilance** is the close repetition of 'c' and/or 's' sounds to evoke all kinds of sounds such as water, whispering, etc. Take this example from Seamus Heaney's 'Mid-Term Break':

  Whispers informed strangers that he was the eldest

- **Rhythm and rhyme** affect a poem's **pace** and make lines **memorable** for easy recall. Read aloud these lines from WH Auden's 'Night Mail' and listen to how the rhythm aids meaning by imitating the steam train that carries the mail:

  This is the night mail crossing the border,
  Bringing the cheque and the postal order [3]

[1] This excerpt from 'War Photographer' is taken from *Standing Female Nude* by Carol Ann Duffy published by Anvil Press Poetry in 1985.

[2] This excerpt from 'Stealing' is taken from *Selling Manhattan* by Carol Ann Duffy published by Anvil Press Poetry in 1987.

[3] This excerpt from 'Night Mail' is taken from *Collected Poems* by WH Auden published by Faber and Faber.

GRADE BOOSTER

Read poetry aloud to discover its rhythm. It's only in the last century or so that people have read silently.

Question Bank 53

1 Alliteration is the repetition, for an effect, of:

   a vowel sounds ☐

   b consonants ☐

   c 'l' sounds only ☐

2 Assonance is the repetition, for an effect, of:

   a consonants ☐

   b 's' sounds ☐

   c vowel sounds ☐

3 Sibilance is:

   a 'c' and 's' sounds close together to suggest a sound ☐

   b 'k' and 'c' sounds close together to suggest a sound ☐

   c words that sound like their meaning ☐

4 Onomatopoeia is:

   a a word that is always very long ☐

   b a word that sounds like its meaning ☐

   c a form of alliteration ☐

5 It's a good idea to read a poem:

   a silently ☐

   b quickly ☐

   c aloud ☐

Poetry Skills: Caesuras

> *If you need to revise **imagery**, have another look at the topic on
> **Shakespeare's imagery** to go over this important skill (see page 94).
> Otherwise, let's take a look at how poetry is punctuated. **Caesuras help to
> convey meaning in poetry.***

A *caesura* literally means 'a cutting'. The plural is caesuras or caesurae. It means a
pause in a line of poetry (called a 'stich'). The term includes any type of
punctuation in a line of poetry. The effect of a caesura is to make a reader
pause, and think about a point or an idea.

When used in the middle of a line the effect can be very meaningful. At the end of
Seamus Heaney's 'Mid Term Break' Heaney remembers the tiny coffin of his
younger brother, who had been killed by a car. The **envoy** (a final single line on its
own) is made more poignant because of the caesura mid-way through the line:

> *A four foot box, a foot for every year.*

Another kind of punctuation in poetry is the 'end stop'. That is, the punctuation of
line endings with full stops, commas, etc.

Question Bank 54

1 What is a caesura?

....

2 What does a caesura signify?

....

3 What is the term for a line of poetry?

....

4 Where would you expect to see a caesura?

....

....

5 Where in a poem might you expect to see an 'envoy'?

....

6 What is the plural of caesura?

....

Poetry Skills: Form 1

> Students often overlook **form** in poetry. As much as **half the meaning** of any poem is present in its form. **Form is the shape and presentation of a poem.**

Many of the forms that follow have been popular for centuries:

- **Ballads** have always been popular with the public because ballads are **dramatic stories** that often feature **ordinary people**. Famous examples include: 'The Rime of the Ancient Mariner' and 'The Ballad of Frankie and Johnny'. Ballads are usually set out in four-line stanzas. They often include a chorus line. Today the form is present in several genres of pop songs.

- **Elegies** are mournful and reflective poems, usually about dead people.

- **Free verse** is composed of stanzas and lines of **irregular length**. It is rather like waves rippling over a shoreline – some lines ripple in further than others, because it is rhythmically natural for them to do so. The form is very popular and it especially suits conversational or argumentative poems. An example is Carol Ann Duffy's 'Valentine'.

- **Lyrical poetry** usually sets out the **thoughts and feelings of a single speaker**. An influential work for today's poets is William Wordsworth and Samuel Taylor Coleridge's *Lyrical Ballads*, published in 1798.

- **Sonnets** are complex poems, usually 14 lines in length. This form is used for the big themes such as love and death.

GRADE BOOSTER

Identify the *form* of the poems you write about because then you'll have a clearer idea of their meaning and purpose.

Question Bank 55

1 .... are often story poems featuring ordinary people.

2 .... poetry is used to set out the thoughts and feelings of a

single person.

3 .... are complex 14-line poems that usually deal with major

themes such as love and death.

4 .... is characterised by lines and stanzas

of irregular length. It is particularly appropriate for argumentative and

conversational poems.

5 .... are reflective poems often written about people who

have died.

6 The form of a poem can contribute up to .... the poem's

meaning.

7 If you identify a poem's form you will have a better idea of a poem's meaning

and ....

Poetry Skills: Form 2

Terms for lines of poetry

Some of these structures will be present in the poems you are studying:

- **Couplets** – these are **two-line stanzas**. They are often rhymed and form a complete unit of meaning. See Simon Armitage's 'About His Person' for unrhymed couplets used to compile a list.

- **Triplets** are **three-line stanzas**. The triplet is a form that naturally lends itself to comic poetry because of its tendency towards longer words and quick rhythm. Seamus Heaney deliberately turned this comic form into a serious one through his **diction** (word choices) and content in 'Mid-Term Break'. Heaney allows the form to revert to its expected rhythm for one line to show that a baby brother was too young to understand the death of an older brother:

  The baby cooed and laughed and rocked the pram
  When I came in, and I was embarrassed
  By old men standing up to shake my hand.[1]

- **Enjambment** or **run-on lines** help evoke **actions** and **movement** in poetry. Enjambment is when the sense of a line runs on into the next one without a pause. Notice the run-on lines beginning *When I came in* and *By old men* in the example above. Run-on stanzas help do similar things.

- **Quatrains** are four-line stanzas of poetry. Historically, this is the most common unit of English poetry.

---

[1] This excerpt from 'Mid-Term Break' is taken from *New Selected Poems* by Seamus Heaney published by Faber and Faber.

GRADE BOOSTER

Be precise: *verse* means the whole poem or collection of poems; *stanzas* are groups of lines within poems.

Question Bank 56

True or false?

1   Couplets are stanzas of three lines.

    ....

2   Couplets are stanzas of two lines.

    ....

3   Triplets are three-line stanzas and are usually associated with comic poems.

    ....

4   Diction means word choices in poetry.

    ....

5   Enjambment and run-on lines are two different things.

    ....

6   Quatrains are five-line poems.

    ....

7   Verse is a term for a whole poem or collections of poems.

    ....

Poetry Skills: Narrative Stance

> *You need to think about whether a poem is narrated in the **first** or **third** person. Let's start by looking at who speaks in poems.*

Who is speaking the poem?

There are two main kinds of speaker: first and third person.

If a poem is narrated **in the first person** the words 'I' and 'me' will be present because the person speaking is **within** the poem. Carol Ann Duffy's 'Stealing' is narrated in the first person. Similarly, 'Before You Were Mine' is an autobiographical poem in which she ponders her mother's life before she had any cares or responsibilities.

Duffy's first-person poems are like **dramatic monologues** in which a speaker is placed in a situation and then dramatically released through what he or she says. Robert Browning wrote some of the most striking dramatic monologues in 'Porphyria's Lover' and 'My Last Duchess' in which murderers dramatically explain their actions.

Narrators looking at what is happening from **outside** are known as **third-person narrators**. Poems written in the third person will use 'he', 'she' or 'they'. Their perspective can be god-like, depending on how much a poet allows them to know and see. Duffy's 'War Photographer' is narrated in the third person by a figure from outside the poem. This allows us to think about the implications of how seriously we consider the photographs that the war photographer brings us.

GRADE BOOSTER

Think about how the choice of narrator can affect the themes and ideas in poems.

Question Bank 57

1 Identify the type of speaker from these extracts: first or third person?

   a *The decade ahead of my loud, possessive yell was the best one, eh?*

   ....

   b *I give you an onion.*

   ....

   c *In his darkroom he is finally alone with spools of suffering set out in ordered rows.*

   ....

   d *I sit in the top of the wood, my eyes closed.*

   ....

   e *From the aeroplane he stares impassively at where he earns his living and they do not care.*

   ....

2 Who sometimes speaks in a dramatic monologue?

   ....

3 Whose perspective can sometimes be described as 'god-like'?

   ....

Poetry Skills: Tone

Students rarely mention tone because it can be difficult to identify. However, if you know what to look for you'll have no problems. Let's start by defining 'tone' in poetry. **Tone is the narrator's attitude towards their subject/topic or audience.**

Tones of voice used on subjects/topics and audiences can be: respectful, angry, cold, determined, humorous, ironic, mocking, persuasive, reflective, resigned, sarcastic, serious, sullen, tragic, warm, etc.

More than one tone may be present in a poem.

A narrator's tone is produced by:

- **Carefully-selected words** that can **create or suggest a mood and atmosphere** within a poem. For example, the persuasively argumentative tone of Carol Ann Duffy's 'Valentine' is produced by single words on lines such as: *Here.*

- The **syntax** (word order) in poems: *Not a red rose or a satin heart.*

- The **rhythm and pace** of lines of poetry can also contribute to tone.

- The **use of irony** – where the speaker implies the opposite of what they are saying. A classic example is Lady Macbeth's order to prepare for King Duncan's visit:

  He that's coming
  Must be provided for.

On the surface, the words mean that the household must provide hospitality for Duncan, but the real meaning is that his murder must be prepared for.

GRADE BOOSTER

Remember that tone can change within a poem. See the last stanza of Carol Ann Duffy's 'War Photographer' for the narrator's *sarcastic* comments about us.

Question Bank 58

1 What does 'tone' mean when discussing poetry?

   ....

2 What is 'syntax'?

   ....

3 True or false? Each poem has only one tone.

   ....

4 True or false? Irony is when the writer or speaker implies the opposite of what
   they are saying.

   ....

5 Describe the tone of a poem you are studying.

   ....

Writing about Anthology Poems

> *What do you need for success in this topic? Here's our list of essentials to get high marks. **Remember that your writing shows your understanding.***

What you know about poetry soon becomes evident when you write about it. When revising and writing about poems try to do the following:

1 **Read the poems at least three times including at least one reading aloud.**

2 **Ask yourself what the poems are about.** Their titles and first lines may give you a clue. But remember, at this stage these are your first impressions of the poems.

3 **Examine how the poet gets their meaning across in the poem.** Look carefully at:

- the style of narration
- form
- diction (choice of language and word order)
- imagery
- themes, messages or ideas
- the tone (of the speaker towards the topic and the audience).

4 **Consider any similarities and differences in**: narrative stances, themes, topics, ideas and imagery, etc., between poems by the same poet.

5 Think about whether you have **changed or altered your views** on the poems. If so, give reasons for these changes.

6 You will also be expected to give **your views** on the poems. If you enjoyed or were bored by them, briefly explain **why.**

Try to anchor your exam answers to **key words and phrases** in the question.

GRADE BOOSTER

Remember that you only have 30 minutes to write about *two poems*. Be selective.

Question Bank 59

1 When you write about a poem, what does it show?

   ....

2 How many times should you read poems before writing about them?

   ....

3 Give **one** of two areas at the beginning of a poem that can help you with its meaning.

   ....

4 When you look at two or more poems, which two general questions should you ask first?

   ....

5 What does 'diction' mean?

   ....

6 Where should you give your views in exam essays?

   ....

7 How much time do you have to write an essay in the exam?

   ....

8 How many poems do you need to write about to get higher than a C grade?

   ....

How to Revise Heritage Poems

> *Once you've understood your group of poems you next need to work out the connections between them. Don't worry if you haven't studied Carol Ann Duffy because the method's the same for any poet.* **You need to make cross-references to other poems if you want to get high grades.**

The following themes and ideas can be found in Carol Ann Duffy's poems. Work out which ones recur in two or more poems.

Here we have provided brief notes on these themes as they appear in 'Before You Were Mine'.

Themes in 'Before You Were Mine'

■ **Change**: her mother's life had once been carefree

■ **Relationships**: grandmother, mother and daughter

■ **Types of love**: possessive – 'before you were mine'

■ **Memories**: sparked by a photograph and recalled by Duffy when aged 10

■ **Outsiders**: the daughter is not part of her mother's youth

■ **People's lives**: mother's life before Duffy

My brief notes on a Duffy poem

Themes in: ....

■ **Change** ....

■ **Relationships** ....

■ **Types of love** ....

■ **Memories** ....

■ **Outsiders** ....

■ **People's lives** ....

GRADE BOOSTER

Apply the checklist to other poems by Duffy. Make a note of which poems are linked with similar themes and ideas.

Question Bank 60

If necessary, adapt these questions to poems that you are studying by substituting themes, etc.

1 Write about how two poems explore the theme of change.

   Consider:

   ■ the type of change explored

   ■ the language used to show change

   ■ how the poem's form and structure contribute to the theme

   ■ your response to the poems.

2 Write about two poems that explore memories.

   Comment on:

   ■ the different kinds of memories

   ■ the different ways memories in each poem are set out

   ■ how language, form and structure affect the treatment of memories

   ■ your response to the poems.

3 Write about any two poems that impressed you.

   Write about:

   ■ the themes and ideas of the poems

   ■ how language and imagery are used in the poems

   ■ what you thought about the poems.

Poetry/Texts from Other Cultures

*The skills you'll need for these poems and texts are almost identical to the ones that you need for English Heritage Poems. These texts are produced by **English speakers from around the world**.*

Whether you study a group of poems or a selection of short stories, the skills that are being examined are the same: the **ability to read, understand and to make cross-references between texts** by showing an **awareness of similar themes and ideas**.

To understand the grading scheme, have another look at the topic on Poetry Grading Criteria. The only real addition is the need to place people and powerful emotions **in the context of local customs and traditions**.

As a quick reference on getting top grades, have a look at this checklist:

- Show that you **understand** texts as you explore them.

- Give a **sustained response** in which you show awareness of writers' purposes.

- **Structure your ideas** as you discuss thoughts and feelings in texts.

- Show how **language and imagery** are used as you comment on texts.

- Use **textual detail to support points and ideas**.

- Be **convincing and imaginative** as you explore texts.

- Show **empathy**. That is, show an appreciation of writers' concerns, ideas and attitudes.

- Give an **honest, reasoned, personal response**.

GRADE BOOSTER
Think about the effect the poet has created with their choice of words. How does this relate to the theme of the poem?

Question Bank 61

True or false?

1   Texts from 'other cultures and traditions' are selected from speakers of English from around the world.

   ....

2   Local customs and traditions are not really relevant to poetry.

   ....

3   Examiners will test your understanding of the texts and want to see cross-references between them on themes, ideas, etc.

   ....

4   You should try to identify the writers' purposes in your answers.

   ....

5   The use of imagery and language is not important for these texts.

   ....

6   You must use textual detail in the form of quotations to support your points when writing about texts.

   ....

7   Examiners expect to see a personal response at the end of your essays.

   ....

Linking the Texts of Other Cultures

This can be tricky. The secret is to note strong similarities and differences between texts. **Links are common ideas, themes or messages in poems or stories.**

The following themes, messages and ideas are present in many texts:

- The importance of **language, dialect and power**.
- The importance of **language for roots and identity**.
- Feelings of being **caught between two cultures**.
- **Beliefs, ritual, customs and tradition**.
- Differences in **attitudes and values**.
- Feelings about **change or lack of change**.
- **Protest** against ideas and attitudes such as racism.
- Thoughts and feelings about **independence**.
- Feelings of **celebration**.

Notes on other themes:

- ....
....
- ....
....
- ....
....

GRADE BOOSTER

Ask the experts. If you're unsure of the links that you could make between your texts, ask your teacher. It's their job to explain things like that.

Question Bank 62

1 You need to look for .... and differences between the

poems/texts.

2 Important links will be themes, messages and .... within

texts.

3 An important set of themes is language, ... and power.

4 Another set of themes includes feelings of being caught between two

....

5 Some poems explore differences in .... and values.

6 Other poems explore the theme of language and how it is linked with roots

and ....

7 You will be expected to make ....-references between

.... poems.

Revising Poems Using Tables

> When you revise your poems or texts you could make a table like the one set out below. We've filled in parts of the chart to start you off.

Finding connections between 'Poems from Other Cultures'

Here we have provided the beginnings of a table showing the links between four poems. We could also have put in a column entitled 'Language and power'.

Make your own table on a large piece of paper, showing the themes that are relevant to the poems you are studying.

Write out the titles of your texts in the first column and your themes and messages in the remaining columns. Make brief notes where appropriate and you will discover which poems are linked by similar themes and ideas.

	Language and identity	Caught between two cultures
'Search for my Tongue' by Sujata Bhatt	first-person narrator; uses metaphor of a plant for mother tongue (roots)	First-person narrator rediscovers her origins through speech
From 'Unrelated Incidents' by Tom Leonard		
'Half-Caste' by John Agard		
'Presents from my Aunts in Pakistan' by Moniza Alvi		Half English and half Pakistani, the narrator rediscovers her origins by wearing bright clothes sent by her aunts

GRADE BOOSTER

Find simple, brief notes and phrases that you made in your 'Anthologies' or exam booklets to help you fill in your table.

Question Bank 63

Foundation Level Exam Practice

1 Write about what two poets find important in their culture.

- ■ Consider what you think each poet finds important.

- ■ Explain what you have learned about each culture.

- ■ Comment on how each poet's language brings out their culture.

- ■ Give your own response to the poems.

2 Choose two poems in which roots is a major theme.

Write about:

- ■ How the idea of roots is brought out in each poem.

- ■ The thoughts and feelings of each poem's narrator.

- ■ The use of language and imagery to explore this theme.

- ■ Your response to the poems.

3 Select two poems in which description is important.

Write about:

- ■ What is described.

- ■ The language and imagery of what is described.

- ■ The ideas brought out by this description.

- ■ What the ideas and description make you think and feel.

Sentence Starters for Poetry

> Sometimes it's difficult to say things in exams. You know what you want to say but you find it difficult to put things in the right way. This page can help by giving you a starting point.

Make a mental note of useful phrases that can help you express your ideas.

Some introductory phrases

- Carol Ann Duffy's 'Stealing' is/appears to be about...

- The poem is narrated in the first/second person. This is appropriate because...

- The form of Duffy's poem is free verse / five-line stanzas of variable length / etc. The form helps readers understand...

Ideas for the main body of an essay

- Duffy's use of language/imagery in ... shows...

- The use of alliteration in ... emphasises the feelings/ideas of...

- The caesura after ... evokes feelings/ideas of...

- 'Search for my Tongue' and 'Presents from my Aunts in Pakistan' both share the idea/theme of...

Phrases for conclusions

- The tone in 'Half-Caste' is... , whereas the tone of....

- To sum up, I would say...

- From reading these poems I have learned...

GRADE BOOSTER

You don't want to sound like a robot so vary phrases to suit your purposes.

Question Bank 64

Higher Level Exam Questions For Paper 2

Notice that little or no help is given for students in bullet points. You'll need to make your own brief essay plans after looking at key words and phrases in the question.

Poets in the English Literary Heritage

1 Write about two poems that particularly impressed you. Explain the features of the poems that you found most impressive.

2 Duffy likes to write about 'outsiders'. Compare Duffy's presentation of 'outsiders' in two of her poems.

Poems from Other Cultures and Traditions

1 Choose two poems in which poets are protesting against ideas and attitudes. What are the poets protesting about and how are their protests presented?

2 Write about two poems in which narrators think about their roots. Examine how thoughts and feelings are shown in the poems.

Wide Reading Assignments

*This coursework assignment is often seen as the toughest assignment of all.
Don't worry – we've broken it down into key points to make it easier.*

A comparison of two texts

One of the texts must be in **prose** (either a short story or a novel) and written
before 1914 and by a **recognised author in the National Curriculum**. The
second text can be in **any genre**, from any period and should be by a **writer of
literary merit**.

What you will be asked to do

Most teachers will have you compare two short stories; some compare parts of
novels with short stories. Others even set parts of novels with acts and scenes from
plays. Your teacher will do what is right for you.

The social and historical contexts

To get a top grade you will be expected to write a paragraph or so on the **social,
historical or cultural settings** of your texts. This is not really difficult. A little
Internet research or a good encyclopaedia will reveal what was happening when
the text was written; your research will also throw more light on themes and ideas
in texts. For example, if you need to find out the historical context of *Tess Of The
D'Urbervilles*, you could look up *the rights and position of women* when Thomas
Hardy first published the novel in the 1880s as well as when he set the novel (the
early 1800s).

GRADE BOOSTER

Ask local experts. Talk to your history teacher if you get stuck!

Question Bank 65

True or false?

1 You have to compare or contrast two texts. ....

2 The older text must be written in verse. ....

3 The older text must be written before 1814. ....

4 The later text can be in any genre. ....

5 A writer of literary merit should have produced the second text. ....

6 You must include a paragraph or two on the historical context of each text.

   ....

7 The historical context of a text may help you understand
   a text's themes more clearly. ....

8 You will not have to do any research. ....

9 History teachers may be able to help you. ....

10 'Context' means a chapter of a text. ....

Wide Reading Grading Criteria

When you know what teachers and examiners are looking for you'll have a much better chance of getting a high grade. Let's take a look at what they expect.

What you need to do for a top grade

You will be assessed on **reading and understanding**. Look carefully at the grading criteria below and apply it to your essays.

Answers within the C to B range are likely to show **insight** when commenting on:

- The **similarities and differences** between texts, noting any **implications** that can be drawn from them; for example, the development of women's rights.

- The texts' **relevance for the present day** and **historical contexts**.

- The **style of writing** (humorous, serious, ironic, etc.) and the **use of structure (plot)** and **characterisation**.

- The writers' use of **language and imagery**.

- **Your views** on the texts, their themes and what you learned.

Answers within the A to A* range will show all of the above plus **analytical skill**s when evaluating:

- The **moral, philosophical, historical and social significance** of texts.

- The **writer's craft** through the use of language for figurative, emotive, and ironic effect, or for implication or suggestion.

- The writers' **significance and achievements within the prose-fiction genre**.

You should also show **originality of interpretation** and **empathy** with the writers' **themes and ideas**.

GRADE BOOSTER

Use the word 'text' when discussing any piece of written work and you'll show the examiner that you know this literary term's meaning.

Question Bank 66

1 The two main skills tested in the wide reading assignment are

.... and understanding.

2 .... means the type of writing a writer uses: ironic, humorous,

emotive, persuasive, informative, etc.

3 .... is a literary term for any piece of writing.

4 A text's historical .... includes the social and historical events

that were taking place when the text was written.

5 The writer's .... is a phrase that describes a writer's use of

language for figurative, emotive and ironic effect, or for implication or

suggestion.

6 .... means kind or type.

Novels Versus Short Stories

*It will help if you're aware of the **differences between novels and short stories**. Then you'll know the key elements that you need to think about.*

Similarities

Novels and short stories can **both** have:

- characters
- dialogue
- narrators
- description, mood and atmosphere
- plots
- settings in the past, present or future as well as settings of place
- themes, ideas and messages.

Differences

Short stories differ from novels because the form's shorter length means that:

- They are usually based on a **specific incident or point in time**.
- They have just **one plot**.
- **Description** needs to be far more **concise**.
- **Description** has to add **meaning** to every part of the story or plot.
- **Striking details and images** are used more often.
- **Dialogue** is shorter and more fragmented.
- **Fewer characters** must often do and say more in less time.

GRADE BOOSTER

Remember that the *form* of a piece of writing usually has an effect on its purpose and content.

Question Bank 67

1 List five things that both novels and short stories have.

....

....

2 Give five important differences between novels and short stories.

....

....

3 Why are there usually fewer characters in short stories?

....

....

4 Why can there be more plots in novels?

....

....

Characterisation

How characters can affect plots

Writers try to develop their characters by:

- Giving **descriptions of how they look and act**. A great deal can be inferred from **what characters say and do** and how other characters **interact** with them.

- Giving characters **names that can be emblematic of (symbolise) their significance** for plots. For example, Pip from Charles Dickens' *Great Expectations* is a name that suggests an image of growth. Pip changes from a boy to a 'gentleman' in the novel.

- Showing how characters' **experiences change them**.

- Giving characters **names that are memorable or unusual**. Sometimes writers prefer to suggest the ordinariness of characters by giving them ordinary names, although such characters usually go on to do memorable things.

- Making the **central character's name the same as the title** of the novel or story. Such characters are known as *eponymous* characters; an example of an eponymous character is Jane Austen's heroine, Emma.

- Making main characters the **first-person narrators** of their stories. However, it is necessary to consider how much they can see and know.

- Directing comments on central characters through an **all-seeing third-person narrator**.

GRADE BOOSTER

Try to identify the main characters of a text as early as possible when you first read it and mark up your text with pencilled notes.

Question Bank 68

True or false?

1 Writers never give their main characters memorable or unusual names.

....

2 Authors sometimes give names to characters
   that have a symbolic significance. ....

3 Much can be inferred from what characters say and do. ....

4 A character can never be a first-person narrator. ....

5 First-person narrators have a better view of
   events and characters than third person narrators. ....

6 The term 'eponymous' means a mouse-like character. ....

7 Third-person narrators can help us understand characters
   through the comments that they make on them. ....

8 Characters usually change in the course of a story
   and this has implications for plots. ....

How Stories are Narrated

As with poetry, **the person telling a story can influence how the message is understood**. This topic is quite easy to understand.

First-person narrators

If a character is **inside** the story and repeatedly using 'I' or 'me' then they are a first-person narrator. The **viewpoint** of this narrator may be restricted as they may not be able to read the thoughts of other characters and only know about events that they can see.

Third-person narrators

The **point of view** of these narrators is always that of someone from outside a story looking at events from above. Key words that identify this type of narrator are 'he', 'she', 'they', etc. **Third-person narrators can know as much as their author wants them to.** This means that they can know about everything that happens, as well as what characters are thinking. A third-person narrator who sees and knows **everything** in a story is called an *omniscient* ('all-knowing') narrator.

Beware – what a narrator thinks is not necessarily what the author thinks.

Show in your writing that you are aware that the narrator is simply a mask for the author. Authors may or may not share the views of their narrators.

GRADE BOOSTER

A good term for what a narrator sees and where they see it from is 'point of view'.

Question Bank 69

Identify the type of narrator from these openings from novels.

1 *ALL THIS HAPPENED, more or less. The war parts, anyway, are pretty much true. One guy I knew really **was** shot in Dresden for taking a teapot that wasn't his. Another guy I knew **did** threaten to have his personal enemies killed by hired gunmen after the war. And so on. I've changed all the names.*

Slaughterhouse 5 by Kurt Vonnegut (1970)

....

2 *Emma Woodhouse, handsome, clever, and rich, with a comfortable home and happy disposition, seemed to unite some of the best blessings of existence; and had lived nearly twenty-one years in the world with very little to distress or vex her.*

Emma by Jane Austen (1816)

....

3 *I wish either my father or my mother, or indeed both of them, ... had minded what they were about when they begot me.*

The Life and Opinions of Tristram Shandy (1759)

....

How to Interpret Dialogue

What characters say to each other can help us understand more about them. Let's take a look at what we can learn from studying dialogue.

Dialogue is from the Greek word for 'conversation'.

Dialogue helps bring novels to life and make characters more vivid. It also breaks up **description** and helps create a sense of **variety** in prose.

Dialogue enables readers to discover:

- the **feelings and personalities** of characters

- whether characters can **see through other characters' motives**, etc.

- characters' use or lack of **irony**

- their main **aims and motives** from the words and phrases that they use

- what characters **think** about their **situations** and about **each other**

- what **we, the readers, think of characters** and whether we are **sympathetic** or lack sympathy towards them

- **themes, ideas and messages** in the story or novel.

Question Bank 70

1 Dialogue is the Greek word for ....

2 Dialogue helps break up .... in novels and stories and can

   create a sense of .... in prose.

3 We can discover the feelings and .... of characters.

4 Readers can find out the aims and .... of characters from the

   words and phrases that they use.

5 Readers can see if characters can .... other characters'

   motives.

6 We can discover what characters .... of their own situations

   and about other characters.

7 Dialogue can help us think about whether we have or lack ....

   towards characters.

Mood and Atmosphere

Description to create a variety of feelings

Writers use mood and atmosphere to highlight the **actions** and **feelings** of characters. It can set the **tone** for a piece of writing and create a sense of expectation in the reader for what is to follow.

Mood and atmosphere can be produced by any combination of the following:

- the use of **adverbs and adjectives**

- the description of **light and dark or colours**

- **diction** (carefully-chosen words)

- **length and variety of sentences**

- the writer's use of **syntax** and unusual word order

- **repetition** of words and phrases

- **monologues and day-dreams**

- a range of **imagery**: similes and metaphors, personification, oxymorons, alliteration, assonance and motifs

- language that evokes the **five senses**

- the **tone of voice of the narrator** and their closeness to the plot's action.

GRADE BOOSTER

Practise by looking again at texts that you studied in class for how writers create mood and atmosphere in highly descriptive passages. These skills will come in handy for the Literature GCSE too!

Question Bank 71

Read the passage below and write a few paragraphs on how Bram Stoker creates a mood and atmosphere of dread and fear.

After a fearful journey to Count Dracula's Castle in Transylvania, Jonathan Harker wonders what the future may hold.

As I stood, the driver jumped again into his seat and shook the reins; the horses started forward, and trap and all disappeared down one of the dark openings.

I stood in silence where I was, for I did not know what to do. Of bell or knocker there was no sign; through these frowning walls and dark window openings it was not likely that my voice could penetrate. The time I waited seemed endless, and I felt doubts and fears crowding in upon me. What sort of place had I come to, and among what kind of people? What sort of grim adventure was it on which I had embarked?

Dracula by Bram Stoker (1897)

....

....

....

....

....

Themes and Ideas in Novels

*Themes are **ideas, messages and issues** that writers explore in their stories. There are hundreds of possible themes, so let's start by looking at themes that often crop up at GCSE.*

Short stories, because of their form, tend to limit themselves to one main theme, whereas novels have the space to explore several major and minor themes.

Here are a few of the themes and ideas explored in some of the short stories set by NEAB:

■ **Change, self-realisation and growing up**: 'The Darkness Out There', 'Superman and Paula Brown's New Snow Suit' and 'The Genius'.

■ **Strained or failed relationships between generations**: 'Flight', 'Your Shoes', 'Kiss Miss Carol', 'The Genius' and 'The Test'.

Themes explored in novels commonly studied for GCSE include:

■ **Change from innocence to experience**: *Great Expectations*

■ **Love and social relationships between men and women**: *Tess of the D'Urbervilles, Pride and Prejudice.*

■ **Ideals and the corruption of power**: *Animal Farm.*

■ **Racism and the importance of independence, roots and family**: *Roll of Thunder Hear my Cry*

These themes are just a sample of what can be found at GCSE. What you must do is find out the theme of the novel or short story that you are studying because this will help you to show greater understanding in essay questions.

GRADE BOOSTER

Remember that themes are often associated with the central characters of novels and short stories.

Question Bank 72

1   What does the term 'theme' mean?

    ....

2   Identify three themes found in short stories.

    ....

3   Identify three themes commonly found in novels at GCSE.

    ....

4   Why is it useful to identify the theme or themes of texts that you are studying?

    ....

5   Why are short stories often limited to one theme?

    ....

6   What are the two main skills tested through prose texts in the wide
    reading assignments?

    ....

Exam Skills: Selecting Information

Much of what you've covered already, especially in the media section of this book, will be useful for the exams. Here are a few more reading skills that will help you achieve high grades.

Scanning and skimming

When you **scan or skim** a text, you run your eyes over it twice as fast as you would normally. This helps you to select the **main ideas and points** in texts. You can establish what is important and what is not. It also helps you get a foothold for understanding. *Scanning* means looking for specific facts, features or sections of a text; *skimming* means reading the whole text quickly.

Skim and scan texts to:

- Quickly determine the text's **main ideas**.

- Find **facts** quickly.

- Find the **topic sentence** of each paragraph (usually the first sentence).

- **Understand information** through chapter headings, main headings and subheadings.

- Find and read carefully the **last paragraph** for **summary information**.

- Find **key information** in tables, charts and boxes.

- **Ignore** parts of texts that have **unnecessary information**.

- Read **exam texts** and **answer questions**.

Practise skimming and scanning to locate the main information in articles in newspapers and magazines because this will increase your skills and speed.

GRADE BOOSTER

Remember to read texts again more slowly for deeper understanding.

Question Bank 73

1 Scanning means:

    a throwing stones out into a lake   ☐

    b being on the Internet for too long   ☐

    c quickly selecting key information in texts   ☐

2 List four reasons for scanning and skimming texts.

....

....

....

....

3 If you skim-read a text, what are you doing?

....

....

Exam Skills: Fact and Opinion

> *There's a question worth several marks in Paper 1 that asks you to list facts and opinions from a passage. Read this page to help you get those marks! The key point is that **facts can be proved; opinions cannot**.*

Facts

Facts:

■ can be checked in reference books and official records

■ are expressed in concrete language or specific numbers

■ are generally agreed upon by everyone.

For example: Manchester United won the Premiership in 2001. Tony Blair is the current Prime Minister of Britain.

Opinions

Opinions are often expressed as comparisons (*more, strongest, less, most, better*, etc.)

For example: Chelsea is a *better* team than Arsenal.

Note, however, that a comparison might be a fact if it can be proved.

Opinions are often expressed using adjectives (*brilliant, vindictive, fair, trustworthy*, etc.)

For example: Spain is a *brilliant* holiday destination.

Opinions are often introduced by verbs that suggest some doubt in the writer's mind.

For example: It *appeared* that Lindsey was delighted.

Caution

Opinions can be made to look like facts. A national newspaper that favours homework might use the results of a survey for a headline like this:

Six in ten parents believe in homework

A newspaper against the idea of homework might use the same information like this:

Four parents in ten think homework doesn't help

How and where such a survey was made will also determine how 'factual' it is.

GRADE BOOSTER

Facts are *objective*. Opinions are *subjective*.

Question Bank 74

Identify five facts and five opinions from the following statements.

a The *Daily Express* is a poor quality newspaper. ....

b *The Guardian* is a broadsheet newspaper. ....

c *The Sun* is more attractive to teenagers than The Mirror. ....

d *The Independent* is the best newspaper for sports coverage. ....

e Journalists who work for tabloids are cleverer
than those who work for broadsheets. ....

f The newspaper with the highest circulation is *The Sun*. ....

g People who write for newspapers are called journalists. ....

h It seems that Jenny reads newspapers and is aware of current affairs. ....

i A distinguishing feature of newspapers is the use of columns. ....

j A big story featured by a single newspaper is called a 'scoop'. ....

Exam Skills: Identifying Unseen Texts

*In Paper 1 the failure to identify the **type** of text you're faced with can cost you marks! If you know the text's **form** you'll find it easier to comment on its purpose and audience. **Different kinds of texts have various purposes and audiences.***

Extracts from these kinds of unseen texts are often set in exams:

- autobiographies
- biographies
- journals
- diaries
- essays
- letters
- travel writing
- leaflets
- newspaper articles
- factual and informative materials.

Questions to ask of texts are:

1   What is the **form and layout** of the text? (a magazine or newspaper article, leaflet, diary, letter, etc.)

2   Does the writer use the **first** (I), **second** (you) **or third** (he/she/they) **person**?

3   What is the writer's **purpose** in the text? (to inform, argue, persuade, entertain, explain and describe, advise, etc.)

4   Who is the **expected audience** for this text? (children under 12, teenagers, young women, middle-aged people, affluent consumers, etc.)

5   How **successful** is the writer in achieving their **aims**?

6   **Do you share the text's values and ideas?** What is your view of the text?

GRADE BOOSTER

This is a crucial topic because it could make the difference between a high exam mark and an average one.

Question Bank 75

Write a couple of paragraphs on this text, pointing out:

- the type of text

- its purpose or aim

- the expected audience.

When I pulled the trigger I did not hear the bang or feel the kick – one never does when a shot goes home – but I heard the devilish roar of glee that went up from the crowd. In that instant, in too short a time, one would have thought, even for the bullet to get there, a mysterious, terrible change had come over the elephant. He neither stirred nor fell, but every line of his body had altered. He looked suddenly stricken, shrunken, immensely old, as though the frightful impact of the bullet had paralysed him without knocking him down. At last, after what seemed a long time – it might have been five seconds, I dare say – he sagged flabbily to his knees. His mouth slobbered. An enormous senility seemed to have settled upon him. One could have imagined him thousands of years old. I fired again into the same spot.

From *Shooting An Elephant* by George Orwell

....

....

....

....

....

Reading Exam Skills: Key Words

*You're more likely to give relevant answers if you understand what's behind exam questions. This page will explain the **key words and phrases** to look for when reading exam questions.*

What words and phrases mean in exam questions

The '**attitude to the reader**' is the tone of voice of the writer. This can be humorous, ironic, persuasive, pleading, etc. It will always be related to the writer's purpose.

'**Compare and contrast**' means explain what is similar and what is different.

'**Convey**' means how a writer gets something across to the readers.

'**Style**' or '**use of language**' means the writer's word choices (diction) and how they use features like emotive words and phrases, description, imagery, alliteration, etc.

'**Visual or graphic style**' or '**presentation**' means how the text is laid out to achieve its purpose. For example, if the text is a magazine article, does it have:

- columns

- headings

- sub-headings

- bold print

- italics

- bullet points

- boxed information

- graphs or pictures, etc.?

GRADE BOOSTER

Avoid saying the language used is 'very good' or 'boring'. This suggests that you have nothing to say. Explain how any presentational devices add to a text's messages or purposes, and you'll get high marks.

Question Bank 76

True or false?

1   The 'attitude to the reader' means the tone of voice of the writer.

   ....

2   To 'compare and contrast' just means to explain what is similar.

   ....

3   To 'convey' means to understand something in a text.

   ....

4   'Style' or 'use of language' refers to the word choices and imagery, etc.
   used by writers.

   ....

5   Bullet points, boxes and italics are devices used by writers to organise and
   clarify points or ideas in their writing.

   ....

6   You can get away with saying that the style of presentation or use of language
   is 'very interesting' or 'hopeless'.

   ....

Writing Exam Skills: Key Words

*In Paper 1 you'll be expected to **argue, persuade or advise**, and in Paper 2 to **inform, explain and describe**. Let's kick off with key words and how you can plan your writing.*

Key words for writing questions

- **Describe** means to set out the characteristics of something, to say what something is like.

- **Explain** means to show knowledge and understanding by giving a detailed account of something.

- **Argue** means to take up a stand on an issue or point of view.

- **Advise** is similar to **inform**: it means to **instruct** someone in something as clearly as possible.

Planning your writing

- **Form**: select the most appropriate form for your writing.

- **Purpose**: this will be related to your form – are you going to advise, persuade, inform, etc.?

- **Audience**: have a clear idea of your audience in mind. Questions often ask you to write for a specific audience.

- **Planning content**: brainstorm a brief plan. You should then number the points in the order that you will make them. If necessary, adapt your plan as you write.

- **Use appropriate language**: formal writing must be written in standard English and have an appropriate register (tone for your audience).

- **Be convincing**: avoid sounding pompous, and argue using texts that you read earlier in the exam to help make your points convincing.

GRADE BOOSTER

Read questions several times for understanding and to make sure your answers are relevant.

Question Bank 77

Paper 1: argue, persuade or advise

(Find articles on the issues raised in these questions on the Internet or in newspapers or magazines.)

1 Write an article on the benefits and dangers of part-time or Saturday jobs for teenagers.

2 Write a letter to a newspaper arguing for or against capital punishment.

3 Write a pamphlet for teenagers in which you give advice on how to care for a two-year-old child. Include lists of 'Dos and Don'ts'.

Paper 2: inform, explain or describe

1 Give a detailed description of someone who is important in your life and explain why they are important.

2 Write a letter to your headteacher explaining the consequences of bullying and what can be done to solve it.

3 Produce a pamphlet for the under-12s explaining the educational advantages of reading challenging texts such as novels and short stories.

Why Punctuate?

Getting the basics right is crucial for success in English. If you can punctuate not just correctly but also expressively, you're well on the way to achieving the grade that you want in English.

Punctuation is the system of marks that we use in writing to express ourselves and to clarify our meaning for others.

When we speak, we 'punctuate' naturally through:

- the pauses in our speech

- the tone of voice that we use

- our use of body language.

It has been estimated that 60% of all communication is through body language: posture, use of eyes, hands, elbows and legs, etc.

Punctuation is therefore very personal!

Writing is **deferred speech**.

Writing has always been a second-hand way of getting our ideas across to others. When someone reads a piece of writing, it is usually some time since it was written, and the writer is rarely there in person to explain it. **So when we write we need to ensure that our meaning can be clearly understood by others. That's why we need to be able to use punctuation well.** We are not able to tell our readers what we mean. Nor will we be able to put our audience right if our meaning is further confused through errors in punctuation.

GRADE BOOSTER

Students who use a wide range of punctuation correctly to express their meaning always stand out from others. They tend to attract higher grades.

Question Bank 78

1 What is punctuation?

....

2 Which is most direct: speech or writing?

....

3 Give two ways that we 'punctuate' speech.

....

4 Give an example of body language.

....

5 Speech is an immediate form of communication. When is writing usually read?

....

6 Why is it important to try to get our punctuation right before others read our work?

....

....

Capital Letters

The assured use of capital letters is important not just for correct English but also for your self-confidence in your writing. Check to see if you remember the rules.

Another name for **capital letters** is **upper case**.

Capital letters are used:

- To **begin sentences or lines of verse**: *To be or not to be.*

- To **introduce speech**: *Anna said, 'Have you heard the latest news?'*

- When **starting letters**: *Dear Sir/Madam*, etc. and for the first line of the letter following this – *Thank you for your interest...*

- For **acronyms** for big organisations such as *ITV, UNESCO, UN*, etc., and for well-known countries such as the *UK* and the *US*. If everybody knows the organisation there is no need for a full stop after each letter.

- For **titles** of books, newspapers, bands, TV programmes, etc.: *Pride and Prejudice, The Star, Westlife, Coronation Street* and *The Bill*.

- For **initials of people's names**: *Natalie, J.K. Rowling*.

- For **titles** when they are part of a person's name: *President Bush, Mrs Robinson*.

- For **proper nouns** (particular people and places): *Sean, Glasgow*.

- For **adjectives derived from proper (specific) nouns**: *English, French, Medieval*.

- For **days of the week, months, holidays and special days**: *Monday, April, Easter, Mayday*.

The personal pronoun always needs a capital I: *Can you tell me what happened yesterday in The Bill as **I** didn't get to see it.*

GRADE BOOSTER

It's important to be accurate with capitals. Get into the habit of *proofreading* your work for the errors that you're prone to making.

Question Bank 79

True or false?

1 Capitals are not needed for titles of books, pop bands,
   TV programmes, films, newspapers, etc. ....

2 Acronyms such as the BBC need capitals. ....

3 Well-known acronyms do not need full stops after each capital letter.

   ....

4 The personal pronoun 'I' should always be a capital letter.

   ....

5 People and places do not need capital letters.

   ....

6 Holidays and days of the week need to begin with a capital letter.

   ....

7 There is no need for capitals in names. ....

8 A capital is needed to introduce direct speech.

   ....

9 Adjectives from proper nouns such as 'Spanish' in 'Spanish onion' need
   a capital.

   ....

Parts of Speech

> *Grammar is steadily making a comeback in schools; so you're bound to impress examiners if you sometimes label parts of speech in your work.*

Words have different jobs in speech.

With over 120 million books sold in over 70 years until the 1920s, *McGuffey Readers* helped generations of Americans learn English grammar. The rhymes below helped them remember **parts of speech**. Could they do the same for you?

A **noun's** the name of anything,
As, *school* or *garden, hoop* or *swing.*

Adjectives tell the kind of noun,
As, *great, small, pretty, white* or *brown.*

Instead of nouns the **pronouns** stand:
Their heads, *your* face, *its* paw,
his hand.

Verbs tell of something being done:
You *read, count, sing, laugh, jump,*
or *run.*

How things are done the **adverbs** tell:
As *slowly, quickly, ill,* or *well.*

Conjunctions join the words together;
As, men *and* women, wind *or* weather.

The **preposition** stands before
A noun; as, *in* or *through* a door.

The **interjection** shows surprise;
As, *Oh!* How pretty! *Ah!* How wise!

The definite and indefinite article

The **definite article** is *the* as in
The cat came in for the night.
This can be inferred as *my* cat.

The **indefinite article** is *a* or *an* as in
A cat came in for the night.
It could be someone else's cat!

GRADE BOOSTER

Learn the rhyme off by heart if it helps you recall parts of speech.

Question Bank 80

1 Adjectives:

   a 'Tell of something being done' ☐

   b 'Tell the kind of noun' ☐

   c 'Join words together' ☐

2 A noun is:

   a 'The name of anything' ☐

   b 'Something being done' ☐

   c Showing 'surprise' ☐

3 Adverbs:

   a 'Stand before a noun' ☐

   b 'Tell how things are done' ☐

   c 'Are something being done' ☐

4 Pronouns:

   a 'Show surprise' ☐

   b 'Stand before a noun' ☐

   c 'Stand instead of nouns' ☐

5 Conjunctions:

   a 'Join the words together' ☐

   b 'Tell how things are done' ☐

   c 'Show surprise' ☐

Types of Sentences

We're not always conscious of the kind of sentences that we write. But if you can identify some sentences in exam passages, that is bound to impress the examiner. Let's start by identifying the four main types of sentence: **statements, exclamations, instructions or commands and questions.**

Statements

These are the most common type of sentence and they **usually give information**:

The girls arrived home at five-thirty.
My name is Ben and I live in Maidstone.
Samantha never gets her homework in on time.

Exclamations

These always show **sudden emotions or feelings**:

Help!
Ouch!
Oh, no!

Instructions or commands

These sentences **tell or command you to do something**:

Dogs must be carried on escalators.
Only one purchase per customer.
Open this way up.

Questions

These are always **requests for information** of some kind:

Where is Donna?
Is she with Theresa?
Did she go out with Dan?

Remember that **rhetorical questions** are not asking for information but rather aim to produce an effect in listeners such as agreement.

How could he get away with saying that?
Is this the kind of world we want for our children?

GRADE BOOSTER

If you can identify kinds of sentences in exams, you'll stand out from the other candidates – and that will lead to a better grade.

Question Bank 81

Identify each sentence using one of the following terms:

- statement
- exclamation
- instruction or command
- question.

1 My name is Gemma. ....

2 Have you got the time on you? ....

3 Hooray! ....

4 Guarantee cards must be presented with cheques. ....

5 Take the Northern Line and then change at London Bridge. ......

6 Where have you been? ....

7 Passengers must present their passports with their tickets at check in. ....

8 Ruth! ....

9 Would you like one too? ....

10 How could anyone refuse such a great offer? ....

How Sentences are Made

> *If you know how sentences are put together, the possibility of producing errors is greatly reduced.* **Words can be grouped in three ways: phrases, clauses and sentences.**

Phrases

Phrases are groups of two or more words and sayings with no verb:
a cheap skate; a whale of a time; a red herring, etc.

Clauses

Clauses are groups of words that include a verb:
the dog barked; the moon shone; the sky darkened; the sun rose, etc.

Sentences

Sentences have at least one clause. Sentences also have a full stop, question mark or exclamation mark to complete them:
Yasmin is the most popular girl in the school. Don't you agree?

Independent clauses and dependent clauses

■ **Independent** clauses can stand on their own as sentences: .
<u>*The girls called out to each other*</u> *before catching the bus for school.*
Since releasing their single, <u>*the band has gone straight to number one.*</u>

■ **Dependent** clauses cannot stand on their own as sentences:
<u>*If you need to save money*</u>*, buy a supersaver ticket.*
You should book these concert tickets early <u>*because the show is bound to sell out.*</u>

GRADE BOOSTER

Dependent clauses can go *before* or *after* a main clause and are often introduced with *after, as, since, because, if,* etc.

172

Question Bank 82

1 What is a clause?

   ....

2 What must a sentence include?

   ....

3 Identify the main clauses in these sentences.

   a As I approached the turn-off for the motorway it began to rain.

   b Amy's father bought her a new car after she passed her driving test.

   c Since getting my new computer I am spending half my life in Internet chat rooms!

4 Identify the dependent clauses in these sentences.

   a I am a great fan of soaps as I love following all the characters' lives.

   b My cat knows when I'm coming home because she recognises the sound of my car.

   c After getting my Saturday job I now have the money to buy new clothes.

5 Give three examples of words that can signal a dependent clause.

   ....

   ....

   ....

Full Stops and Sentences

> *The full stop is the main punctuation mark that completes a sentence.*
> **Full stops signal the end of one idea and the beginning of another.**

The expressive use of full stops

Full stops are the commonest mark for ending sentences; however, when they are used in an **expressive** way they can be very effective. If you want readers to slow down and mull over what you have written, it is better to use a full stop rather than a semi-colon or a colon.

Varying sentence lengths

Different styles can be achieved through varying the length of sentences.

The length of sentences should be appropriate for what you are saying. Sentences that describe or explain something may be longer and divided by semi-colons because they can be read at speed. Shorter sentences slow readers down and are best suited for important points and dramatic impact.

Aim to vary your style of punctuation

This means **varying the punctuation that you use**: full stops, semi-colons, colons, exclamations and question marks. Read on to find out more about how to use colons and semi-colons.

GRADE BOOSTER

Students who vary their punctuation and sentences stand out from the rest.

Question Bank 83

True or false?

1 Full stops are an uncommon way of ending sentences.

   ....

2 Full stops used in an expressive way can be very effective.

   ....

3 The skill of varying your sentence length will help you get good grades.

   ....

4 Sentence length does not have to be appropriate for what you are writing.

   ....

5 Putting in semi-colons slows the reader down.

   ....

6 If you always write long sentences it shows that you are clever.

   ....

7 Students who vary their style of punctuation and sentence length show more
   control over their writing.

   ....

Commas

Commas do many helpful jobs in sentences, but ending sentences is not one of them! Commas help prevent confusion by making your meaning clear. Let's start by looking at the main uses of commas. **Commas mark off words and phrases in sentences.**

Commas can be used in the following ways:

- To separate words, phrases and connectives in sentences:
  The students worked hard, revised thoroughly and deserved their excellent results.

- To separate items in a list:
  Sarah went to her local supermarket and bought: a half dozen eggs, a loaf of bread, two pints of milk, two packets of biscuits and a chocolate gateau.

  Notice that we don't usually put a comma before *and*, unless not doing so would create confusion.

- To clarify sentences that would otherwise be misleading:
  When eating, a person should use good manners.

- To separate direct speech from the rest of the sentence:
  Ian whispered anxiously to Ruth, 'How far have you got with your essay?'

GRADE BOOSTER

When you want to insert extra information or comments into a sentence, commas are needed to make your meaning clear.

Question Bank 84

1 Put the commas in these sentences to make their meaning clear.

   a When you go to the shops please buy me: three packets of chewing gum two bags of cheese and onion crisps a Mars Bar and a can of coke.

   b 'It's too far to walk' said Jade wearily. James replied 'Come on Jade; it's only one more mile.'

   c Stuart who is five years younger than Sam is the baby of the family.

2 Give three important uses for commas.

....

....

....

3 Where should you never put a comma?

....

....

Colons

This is a colon:

How colons are used

■ **To introduce lists:**

When you go on the camping trip bring: a sleeping bag, rations for two days, matches, a torch, a compass, walking boots, etc.

■ **To introduce speech in plays:**

Rita: Why did you do it?

■ **Before information that explains what you have just written:**

John helped win the match: he scored two goals.

■ **To introduce longer quotations that are separated from your writing:**

When Romeo sees Juliet at night by her window he shows his feelings for her through his imagery of light:

Romeo: But soft, what light through yonder window breaks?
It is the east and Juliet is the sun!

GRADE BOOSTER

As with other punctuation marks, make sure that when you use colons they add expression to your writing.

Question Bank 85

1 Write a colon. ....

2 Put in colons where they are needed for expression or sense in the following extracts.

   a Can I have two cheese sandwiches, a slice of gateau, a cup of coffee and two serviettes please?

   b Macbeth, on being told of the death of his wife, faces his own mortality and considers how all his evil efforts seem to have been in vain

     Life's but a walking shadow, a poor player
     That struts and frets his hour upon the stage
     And then is heard no more. It is a tale
     Told by an idiot, full of sound and fury,
     Signifying nothing.

   c Krystle worked hard for her exams she got four A*s and four As.

3 Give four ways that colons can be used.

....

....

....

....

Semi-Colons

Semi-colons are a great substitute for full stops because you can use them for a variety of purposes. They open up a range of expressive possibilities in your writing. Let's see why. **Semi-colons create shorter pauses than full stops.**

This is a semi-colon ;

- A semi-colon creates more of a break than a comma, but less of a break than a full stop.

- Semi-colons can link related or equal statements.

  You can end a sentence with a full stop; or you can link it to the next sentence with a semi-colon.

  The sun rose; the birds began to sing.

  Geoff is great at school; he's awful at home.

- Semi-colons are also used to link short statements.

  Fog descended on the scene; it became dark; light rain began to fall.

  The house was immense; it had six bedrooms; there were also two bathrooms on different floors.

- Semi-colons are used to separate items in a list when it would be confusing to use commas (because there are commas within the list items).

  When you check in for your flight please bring: a valid passport for travel; your flight tickets; all the luggage you are checking in; rucksacks, handbags and similar hand luggage.

Note that you do *not* need a capital letter after using a semi-colon.

GRADE BOOSTER
Semi-colons are very good for descriptive or informative writing where you want readers to read through your text quickly.

Question Bank 86

1 Make sense of these related statements by adding semi-colons.

   a Both sides were equally drawn it was one-one at half time.

   b The twins have different personalities Bianca loves talking and Alan hardly says a word.

   c To err is human to forgive, divine.

2 Insert the semi-colons between these short descriptive statements.

   a I rose at 7am I ate a full breakfast I then got the car out of the garage and went to work.

   b Go on holiday and enjoy yourselves we will look after the house.

   c It was a very cold night the cat looked anxiously at the door.

3 Use semi-colons to separate the instructions in this list.

To get to the ice rink: take the first turn on your left at Sainsburys go half-way up Treetop Hill go left at the traffic lights by the Red Lion and you're there.

Quotation and Title Marks

*In English at GCSE level you will need to know how to punctuate quotations and titles in your work. It's really easy once you know the rules. **Quotation and title marks are inverted commas used around titles or direct speech.***

Quotation marks

Whatever you do, be consistent. When you write, stick to single or double quotation marks.

George Bernard Shaw said, 'The golden rule is that there are no golden rules'.

The last words of Queen Elizabeth I were "All my possessions for a moment of time".

Title marks

The convention in secondary schools is to use inverted commas for book titles, newspapers, stories, magazine titles, television programmes, films, shows, etc. For example:

'Gladiator' is a movie.

'The Sun' is a newspaper.

The use of inverted commas is also an important way of distinguishing an eponymous character from the **title of a play or a novel**.

Macbeth is a character and 'Macbeth' is the play.

Emma is a character and 'Emma' is the title of Jane Austen's novel.

In word-processed work, if you put the title of a text or film in *italics* there is no need to use inverted commas.

Romeo and Juliet, The Mirror, An Inspector Calls, The Big Issue, etc.

GRADE BOOSTER

Proofread your work to check you've put inverted commas around titles of texts. It's attention to detail that gets you marks.

Question Bank 87

1 What do quotation or title marks look like?

....

2 Should you vary your style of quotation marks or remain consistent?

....

3 Is the convention in secondary schools to underline titles or to put inverted commas around them?

....

4 How should you distinguish the title of a text from its eponymous character?

....

5 In word-processed work, how else can you distinguish a text's title?

....

6 When you complete any piece of written work, what should you do?

....

The Rules of Direct Speech

Many students lose marks every year because they're unsure of how to set out direct speech. You can avoid being one of them. There are only a few rules and it's possible to learn them by heart.

How direct speech is set out

There are four main rules:

1   The words spoken should be in either single or double **inverted commas**:

    Sophie asked, 'Have you got the time?'

    Remember that you need to be consistent in your choice of single or double inverted commas.

2   Direct speech must be **separated** from the rest of the writing by **any punctuation mark**. This is most commonly a comma. Note the comma after 'asked' in the example above.

3   You must use a capital letter when beginning direct speech.

    Jade angrily asked her brother, Andrew, ' Why did you give my 'Shaggy' CD to Jessica?'

4   Each time you **introduce a new speaker** you must **begin a new line** and, unless you are using a word-processor, **indent it**. *Indent* means begin your writing three letter spaces in from the margin:

    Andrew replied, 'Jessica told me that she'd lend me her copy of her Gorrillaz CD'.

    'That's no excuse. In future, lend her your own CDs and not mine!' said Jade.

    Note that inverted commas are **not** needed for **reported speech**:

    She told him off for giving her CD to Jessica.

GRADE BOOSTER

Vary your use of direct speech. You can do this by sometimes putting *who* **is speaking and** *how* **they are speaking** *at the end of direct speech* **instead of at the beginning.**

Question Bank 88

1 How many main rules are there for setting out direct speech?

    a   seven   ☐

    b   four   ☐

    c   fourteen   ☐

2 How should direct speech be separated from other writing?

    a   by any form of punctuation   ☐

    b   by commas only   ☐

    c   by colons only   ☐

3 You need to use a capital letter:

    a   two words before the direct speech begins   ☐

    b   for the first word of direct speech   ☐

    c   only for adverbs in direct speech   ☐

4 Inverted commas are needed:

    a   to begin and end direct speech   ☐

    b   only at the end of direct speech   ☐

    c   only at the beginning of direct speech   ☐

5 You need an indented new line each time:

    a   you continue with the same speaker   ☐

    b   you change a speaker   ☐

    c   you feel like it   ☐

Apostrophes of Possession

This is another area where mistakes are often made. If you're not wholly sure about apostrophes of possession, read the topic and try the questions. Once you know the basics, possessive apostrophes are simple.
Apostrophes of possession show ownership.

- The apostrophe **for a single owner** is usually placed **before the final *s***:

  Alex Stuart's car; Melissa's hi-fi system; the window's frame, etc.

- Apostrophes **for several owners** are usually placed **after the final *s***:

  the Stuarts' car; the sisters' hi-fi system; the windows' frames

- **Exceptional owners**: if the name of a single owner already ends in an *s* you should either place the apostrophe after the final *s* or add another *s* and place the apostrophe between the two.

  James' personal stereo **or** *James's personal stereo*

Whichever method you use, remember to be **consistent**.

- For **joint owners** the apostrophe can be put in the **last word**:

  James and Judith's stereo

- When a **plural noun has an ending other than *s*,** the apostrophe must go before the *s*:

  the men's silk ties; the women's shoes; the children's toys

- *It's* and *its* can be a source of errors.

  It's is short for *It is* and so needs an apostrophe:

  It's a fine day.

  But *its* is a possessive pronoun that does not need an apostrophe:

  Lead your dog over to the window and I'll take its picture.

GRADE BOOSTER

You can vary your expression and avoid possessive apostrophes by writing things the long way round. For example, the long way to say *the bird's wings* is *the wings of the bird*.

Question Bank 89

True or false?

1 Apostrophes cannot show ownership.

....

2 Apostrophes for single owners usually go before the final *s*.

....

3 With two owners whose names follow each other, the apostrophe goes before the final *s* of the second owner.

....

4 The apostrophe for several owners usually goes after the final *s*.

....

5 When a noun has a plural ending other than s, the apostrophe must go before the *s*.

....

6 Which of the following sentences are correct?

   a The firemen's meeting went on for an hour.

   b Childrens' games like hide and seek are always popular.

   c They were voted the people's favourite band.

Apostrophes of Omission

*Another important use for apostrophes is to **indicate letters or words that have been abbreviated or shortened**. Revise your knowledge of this use of apostrophes and you'll have this topic covered.*

Apostrophes that show letters and words are missing

The main uses for apostrophes of omission are:

■ For informal or casual language such as dialect:

   'I'm always doing the washing up! It's your turn, isn't it?'

   "'Ere, are yer comin' or not? We'll be late for the match!'

■ For writing the time:

   'Let's meet at six o'clock' (six of the clock).

■ In lines of verse where poets want to leave out a syllable to keep the rhythm even:

   She dwelt upon th' untrodden ways. (Wordsworth)

■ In plays or novels for direct speech to make dialect and speech appear realistic:

   Rita to Frank: I'm comin' in, aren't I? It's that stupid bleedin' handle on the door. You wanna get it fixed!' (From *Educating Rita* by Willy Russell)

GRADE BOOSTER

Remember to avoid using abbreviated words and phrases in formal writing such as essays and letters to people that you don't know. They should only be used in informal, friendly pieces of writing.

Question Bank 90

1 What do apostrophes of omission show?

....

....

2 Give four instances where you would expect to find or use apostrophes
   of omission.

....

....

3 Place apostrophes in these sentences to make them correct.

   a Whats the matter? Dont you feel well?

   b Wed have gone to the party if theyd asked us to come.

   c Lets get cracking because weve got a lot to do.

   d Its time to give the cat its medicine.

Paragraphing Skills

*Paragraphing skills are important for your development as a writer. It's also useful to know how professional writers develop their points and ideas in paragraphs. Let's start by defining what paragraphs are. **Paragraphs are sections or passages in a piece of writing.***

A new paragraph signifies that the writer has moved on to a new idea.

When you write a piece of **fiction** you need a new paragraph each time you:

- change a place or setting
- change a speaker
- change the time
- change the viewpoint
- want to make an effect.

In **non-fiction** you will need a new paragraph each time you:

- change a topic
- make a new point within a topic
- change the time
- change the viewpoint.

Each paragraph has a topic sentence that is usually, although not always, the first sentence of a paragraph. The rest of the paragraph expands upon the main idea in the topic sentence. Sentences also have a **topic word** from which the sentence takes its meaning. Take this introductory paragraph from a leaflet by 'World Vision Child Sponsorship'. The topic word has been highlighted.

*Would you **drink** a glass of filthy water? Almost certainly you wouldn't. And you wouldn't let a child drink it either.*

GRADE BOOSTER

If you break your writing up into logical paragraphs, you make it easier to follow and understand.

Question Bank 91

Why do each of these sentences begin a new paragraph? Is it because of a new topic, time, place or speaker?

1   *I must have been asleep, for certainly if I had been fully awake I must have noticed the approach of such a remarkable place.*

    ....

2   *I stood in silence where I was, for I did not know what to do.*

    ....

3   *'Welcome to my house! Enter freely and of your own will!'*

    ....

4   *'I am Count Dracula; and I bid you welcome, Mr. Harker, to my house.'*

    ....

5   *The Count himself came forward and took off the cover of a dish, and fell to at once on an excellent roast chicken.*

    ....

6   *It is again early morning, but I have rested and enjoyed the last twenty-four hours.*

    ....

7   *When I found I was a prisoner a sort of wild feeling came over me.*

    ....

From *Dracula* by Bram Stoker.

Spelling Methods

Many students have difficulty with spelling. But help is at hand. Here are some ways to improve your spelling and impress the examiner.

Ways of improving spelling

Try the following and see which ones work best for you:

- **Look the word up in a dictionary.** Words are alphabetically arranged so all you need is to know your alphabet!

- **Look – say – cover – write – check.** Look at the word correctly spelt. Say it aloud. Cover it up and write it from memory. Then check if you were right.

- **Write a crazy memorable sentence with the word's letters** (a mnemonic). For example, for *guess*: Great Udders Easily Slip Slop. Reserve this method for words you never get right.

- **Sound out the words as you spell them.** Work your way through each syllable to get the word right: *On/o/mat/o/poe/ia*.

- **Think about word patterns and families of words.** Work out how words follow the spelling patterns of other words. For example: *appear, disappear, disappearance, reappear*.

Tricky plural endings

If a noun **ends with y** and has a **consonant before the y**, leave off the y and add *ies* to make the plural:

diary – diaries   curry – curries   company – companies.

However, if the **letter before the y is a vowel**, just add an *s* to make the plural:

boy – boys   journey – journeys   key – keys.

A rule for *i* and *e* in the middle of words

Remember the rhyme: *i* before *e*, except after *c*:

retrieve

but receive

GRADE BOOSTER
Make a list of the words that you continually misspell and learn them.

Question Bank 92

With a friend, test each other on these spellings. Then use the method that suits you best to learn the ones you got wrong.

150 of the trickiest spellings

accelerator
accept (agree to)
except (exclude)
acquire
allowed (let)
aloud (out loud)
a lot (two words)
answer
arguing
argument
appearance
audience
banned
before
beginning
behaviour
believable
believe
beware
bored (fed up)
board (piece of
    wood)
break (shatter)
brake (slow down)
calm
careful
cemetery
character
climbed
collage (artwork)
college (for
    education)
comma
compare
complete
completely
conjunction
cue (for actors)
queue (line of
    people)
cupboard
dangerous

debt (money owed)
dept. (short for
    department)
decide
definitely
devastating
different
disappear
disappointment
disguise
doesn't
don't
effectively
embarrass
excellent
excited
extremely
fair (just)
fare (ticket)
fault
finally
foreign
fought
goodbye
grammar
guess
hypocrisy
imagine
independence
individual
intelligence
interested
intriguing
jealous
kept
knew (past of to
    know)
new (unused)
knife
knives
lead (to lead, or
    metal)

led (past tense of
    to lead)
lounge
lying
lie (to tell a lie)
lie or lay (on a bed)
laid (past of to lay)
leisure
metaphor
minutes
necessarily
necessary
necessity
only
partner
peculiar
people
piece
planned
polite
possess
probably
practice (noun, 'here
    is some spelling
    practice')
practise (verb, 'to
    practise the violin')
preferred
principal (head
    teacher)
principle (point of
    honour)
privilege
probably
proceed
professional
putting
quiet (silence)
quite (a little)
racism
receive
recommend

rehearse
relevant
relieved
restaurant
rhyme
rhythm
right (correct/
    direction)
write (with a pen)
sense
sentence
separate
seriously
sincere
sincerely
skilful
special
squashed
squeaky
stories
straight
succeed
surprise
there (place)
their (ownership)
they're (they are)
tired
toilet
tongue
tragedy
truly
trustworthy
twelfth
unnecessary
until/till
vehicle
weather (rain, etc.)
whether (or not)
weird

Question Bank Answers

Question Bank 1
1 speaking and listening, reading and writing
2 b 20%
3 Shakespeare; a comparison of two texts; the media
4 One text must be in prose, written before 1914 and by an author recognised in the National Curriculum.
5 60%
6 Writing to describe, explain or inform and to argue, persuade or advise.

Question Bank 2
1 true
2 true
3 false
4 true
5 true
6 false
7 false

Question Bank 3
1 for fluency of speech
2 the appropriate tone of voice
3 Standard English
4 To carry forward the points of others and respond to complex speech.
5 maintaining a standpoint or argument
6 A rhetorical question is a question that you are asking without really wanting an answer. It aims to prod an audience into agreeing with you.

Question Bank 4
1 b and d
2 It is spoken by anyone who needs to speak formally: business people, teachers, lawyers, newscasters, etc.
3 It helps them understand each other.
4 It is polite to use it.
5 the East Midlands

Question Bank 5
1 false
2 false
3 true
4 true
5 false for a, b, c and d

Question Bank 6
1 b
2 c
3 b
4 a
5 c

Question Bank 7
1 explain, describe or narrate; explore, analyse or imagine; or discuss, argue or persuade
2 to help your structure, fluency and self-confidence
3 libraries, local experts, the Internet, etc.
4 cards or spider diagrams
5 in front of a mirror or with a friend

Question Bank 8
1 b
2 a
3 c
4 a
5 b

Question Bank 9
1 not made up
2a false
b true
c false
3 purpose, audience and content
4 to explain, describe, persuade, instruct, advise, etc.
5 Use appropriate punctuation, word choices and sentence structure.

Question Bank 10
1 For better structure and detail.
2a audience
b purpose
c form
3 It's easier to find your place and saves time when writing.
4 two including your best
5 Check for errors.

Question Bank 11
1 key words and phrases
2 brainstorm, spider diagram
3 three or four stages
4 evidence in the form of brief quotations
5 Plan your final essay on one sheet of paper.

Question Bank 12
1 historical context
2 topic
3 beginning
4 quotations
5 essay title
6 connectives (or linking phrases)
7 views

Question Bank 13
1 Examine key words and phrases in assignments and re-read the relevant chapters or parts of texts.
2 characters, themes, imagery, mood and atmosphere, plots, etc.
3 a pencil and a sheet of blank paper
4 the first five minutes
5 Add images and colours.
6 Link them together with lines so you can see connections.

Question Bank 14
1a words that emphasise points
b words to introduce examples
c words to add points or ideas
d words to argue and make points
2 speaker

Question Bank 15
1 What is the same and what is different?
2a contrast
b compare
c sum up
3 the main sentence that identifies the focus of that paragraph
4 near the beginning
5 linking words that connect ideas
6 no

Question Bank 16
1 yes
2 explore, imagine and entertain
3 audience
4 1000 words
5 to hold an audience's interest / get a good grade
6 the ability to use punctuation and expression to achieve effects
7 the attitude and voice of the narrator

Question Bank 17
1 Clear it with your teacher first.
2 story poems, often about ordinary people
3 with a twist in the tail
4 Write extra scenes or an episode.
5 Proofread for errors.

Question Bank 18
1 false
2 true
3 true
4 false
5 true
6 true
7 true

Question Bank 19
1 from within the story
2 a clear beginning, middle and end
3 kind or type of story
4 Time is chronological; straightforward; events are told in the order in which they happened.
5 Time is not straightforward. Flashbacks are used.

6 a moral or a twist in the tale
7 at or near the beginning
8 an unusual description of a setting, character or incident

Question Bank 20
1 c
2 b
3 b
4 b
5 c

Question Bank 21
1 to set out or tell about something in words
2 It makes subjects and settings more realistic.
3 sight, touch, hearing, taste and smell
4 It encourages the reader to use their imagination.
5 the end
6 It can bore readers, sound stilted, slow down the pace, etc.

Question Bank 22
1 an unnecessary repetition of meaning already expressed
2 *Despite playing* (or *Although they played*) *badly the team won the match.*
3 wholly
4a because or since
b he
c now
5 They are ambiguous and lack clarity. They could mean something different from what the writer intended!
6 having more than one possible meaning

Question Bank 23
1a Many
b Few
c She is
2 an overworked simile or metaphor
3 They are *all* clichés!
4 You choose.

Question Bank 24
1a reading
b comment

2 the pronoun 'I'
3a false
b true
c false
d true
e true
f true
g false

Question Bank 25
1 under a picture
2 the main story on the front page
3 the paper's or magazine's
4a punch line
b who, what, when, where, why
c a feature
5 in the final exams

Question Bank 26
1 false
2 true
3 false
4 true
5 false
6 false
7 true
8 true
9 true
10 true

Question Bank 27
1 leaflets, pamphlets, flyers, articles
2 the repetition of a consonant for effect
3 to emphasise a message or make a product sound exciting
4 the repetition of vowel sounds for effect
5 a catch phrase associated with a product or service
6 to persuade readers through leading them to feel emotions such as sympathy and empathy
7 People can relate to accounts from a specific person.
9 in the final exams

Question Bank 28
1 b
2 c
3 a
4 b
5 a

Question Bank 29

1 true
2 false
3 true
4 true
5 true
6 true
7 false

Question Bank 30

1 To make a company or brand easy to recognise, to inspire trust .
2 They help readers quickly understand main points.
3 They can break up blocks of text; images show who you can help (in charities' publicity).
4 Captions describe pictures and provide interpretations of them.
5 It can carry deep symbolic associations for readers.
6 To persuade us to buy their product or service.

Question Bank 31

1 a
2 b
3 a
4 a
5 b

Question Bank 32

1 atmosphere
2 filler lights
3 key light
4 back light
5 filler lights
6 filler light
7 tone

Question Bank 33

1 how space is used
2 colour, font and type size, graphics and space
3 It may have a symbolic significance or an association.
4 The choice of font can emphasise messages about the product.
5 graphs, charts, etc.
6 Space around a product is either filled or unfilled.
7 Point, evidence, comment.

Question Bank 34

1 a and c
2 b
3 b
4 a
5 b

Question Bank 35

1 storyline or outline
2 Kind or type of story such as romance, adventure, etc.
3 They have limited time in which to establish a character.
4 place and time
5 Beliefs such as family values, saving money, etc.
6 The audience that the commercial is aimed at.
7 As many appropriate technical terms as you can.

Question Bank 36

1 true
2 true
3 false
4 true
5 false
6 true
7 true
8 false

Question Bank 37

1 setting or place
2 establishing
3 mid or half
4 close-ups
5 total or long shot
6 close-ups
7 point of view

Question Bank 38

1 a change of time or scene
2 vulnerable
3 It makes them seem impressive and strong.
4 Rapid editing; it is a quick succession of shots.
5 Everything that is in the frame, particularly the setting.
6 One scene is 'wiped' from the frame by another.
7 The camera moves from one place to another.
8 two

Question Bank 39

1 true
2 false
3 true
4 true
5 true
6 false
7 true

Question Bank 40

1 three
2 rhymed verse
3 poetic verse
4 blank verse
5 dramatic
6 language
7 sonnets

Question Bank 41

1 unrhymed verse
2 characters of elevated rank
3 the rhythms of everyday speech
4 iambic pentameter
5 five
6 one
7 the first unstressed, the second stressed
8 It can momentarily reverse the rhythm.
9 For an expressive reason such as a moment of drama.
10 blank verse

Question Bank 42

1 c
2 a
3 b
4 a
5 b

Question Bank 43

1 true
2 false
3 false
4 true
5 false
6 true
7 true
8 false
9 true
10 true

Question Bank 44

1 a dramatic monologue or soliloquy
2 a character's thoughts and state of mind
3 do/say

196

4 change
5 change or develop
6 directions
7 profiles

Question Bank 45
1 a
2 b
3 a
4 a
5 b

Question Bank 46
1 the beginning and end
2 usually Act 2
3 the climax
4 murders, disgrace, etc.
5 Rightful order is resumed and lessons are learned, etc.
6 People were going through a period of uncertainty over the royal succession.
7 He sometimes juxtaposes a serious scene with a comic one.

Question Bank 47
1 b
2 c
3 b
4 b
5 c
6 a

Question Bank 48
1 message or idea
2 a time of change in Shakespeare's society
3 Very often they are punished.
4 *Julius Caesar, Romeo and Juliet, The Merchant of Venice, Henry IV, Parts 1 and 2, Henry V,* and several others
5 fate or fortune
6 To understand the play more fully.

Question Bank 49
1 b
2 a
3 b
4 b
5 b

Question bank 50
1 clear planning
2 usually early in your essay but it can go anywhere
3 secret or arranged marriages; vendettas, etc.
4 blank verse
5 It is more elevated and dignified.
6 yes
7 yes

Question Bank 51
1 British
2 reading and understanding
3 topics
4 15
5 30
6 themes
7 links

Question Bank 52
1 false
2 true
3 true
4 false
5 true
6 false
7 true

Question Bank 53
1 b
2 c
3 a
4 b
5 c

Question Bank 54
1 any punctuation that breaks up a line of poetry
2 a pause to emphasise something or make meaning clear
3 a stich
4 It can appear anywhere in a line of poetry.
5 at the end of a poem
6 caesuras or caesurae

Question Bank 55
1 ballads
2 lyrical
3 sonnets
4 free verse
5 elegies
6 half
7 purpose or aim

Question Bank 56
1 false

2 true
3 true
4 true
5 false
6 false
7 true

Question Bank 57
1 a first person
  b first person
  c third person
  d first person
  e third person
2 a first-person narrator
3 a third-person narrator

Question Bank 58
1 the narrator's attitude towards their subject or audience
2 word order
3 false
4 true
5 Check your answer with a friend or teacher.

Question Bank 59
1 your understanding of a poem
2 at least three times
3 its title and the first sentence
4 What is the poem about? How does the poet get their meaning across?
5 the poet's choice of words
6 at the end of your essay
7 30 minutes.
8 two

Question Bank 60
1 The best poems to write about here are 'Before You Were Mine' and 'In Mrs Tilcher's Class'. These are autobiographical poems in which Duffy reflects on her memories from when she was about ten. In the first poem change is explored through Duffy examining a photograph and imagining the carefree life that her mother led before Carol was born. Duffy's use of the present tense gives a feeling of immediacy for her memories. Images of mid-1950s Glasgow are evoked with George Square (a

famous meeting point for a night out) and the movie star whose name her mother shares, 'Marilyn'. Look out for striking images where Duffy uses several of the five senses to give her reflections a sense of realism. Free verse is an appropriate form for Duffy's reflections on her mother's past.

Duffy also uses the five senses 'In Mrs Tilcher's Class' for similar effect. The poem charts her last year in primary school. This is also the year in which she learns the facts of life. The poem explores the changes that spark the onset of adolescence. The first two eight-line stanzas present a reassuringly unchanged world of the protective Mrs Tilcher and school life. The last two stanzas have only seven lines and introduce a discordant note through their lack of harmony. The narrator not only feels change in the outside world but also within her own body. Look out for sexual images and word choices (diction) that suggest change and uncertainty in these final stanzas.

2 Again, 'Before You Were Mine' and 'Mrs Tilcher's Class' are ideal for this question. You could also try 'War Photographer' and 'Stealing'. If you choose these last two poems you could write about the photographer's memories of his latest photographs; examine also how the photographer feels and behaves in each setting: the country where he took the photographs and England where he develops them. The poem is dramatically written in the present tense and set out in four six-line stanzas; the form imposes a sense of regularity for what is an unusual job. Notice how the

cycle begins again as the photographer leaves for another assignment. The poem's third-person narrator uses a respectful tone to describe the photographer. Its diction emphasises the photographer's isolation and the religious nature of his duty to the dead.

'Stealing' examines the motives and desires of its first-person narrator thief. Its five stanzas give the poem a distinctive lack of harmony. The jerky, defensive monologue of the thief, who could be of either sex or any age, fits in with the form. Notice how the contrasting subjects of each poem are isolated figures who share highly developed visual skills. Remember to use brief quotations to prove your points!

Question Bank 61
1 true
2 false
3 true
4 true
5 false
6 true
7 true

Question Bank 62
1 similarities
2 ideas
3 dialect
4 cultures
5 attitudes
6 identity
7 cross, two

Question Bank 63
1, 2 The general answer below could help with question 1 and/or 2. Remember to use brief quotations to prove your points.
Moniza Alvi's 'Presents from my Aunts in Pakistan' and Grace Nichols' 'Hurricane Hits England' show how either clothes or the weather can put the poets in touch with their roots and ease concerns over

uncertainty in their lives. Notice how Moniza Alvi's colourful and highly-decorated clothes, sent by her aunts from Pakistan, help her to establish the Pakistani half of her identity; in comparison British clothes seem plainer and less ornate. The 'prickly heat' and the 'conflict' of the 'fractured land' of her father contrasts with that of Britain. The Great Storm that hit England in 1987 reminds Grace Nichols of the terrific hurricanes that usually occur in the Caribbean. The storm reminds her of her West Indian roots and the weather gods of her African ancestors as she considers the mystery of how such a storm could cross the globe to England. The storm helps connect Grace not only with her roots but also with her host country, England, which she did not feel part of before. She learns that the earth is not so big after all. She concludes, 'That the earth is the earth is the earth'.

3 Good choices here would be 'Ogun' by Edward Kamau Braithwaite and 'Blessing' by Imtiaz Dharker. The narrator of 'Ogun' celebrates the skills and craftsmanship of his 'uncle' but then goes on to show how these skills were no longer required when mass-produced furniture destroyed his uncle's furniture business. 'Blessing' is another poem that has celebration as its theme, in which a municipal pipe bursts and the scorched local people take advantage of this 'blessing' to share water. Both poems are highly descriptive, use a wide range of sensual imagery and include metaphors and similes to articulate the plight or joy of their subjects. The poems also rely on onomatopoeia and carefully-chosen diction to emphasise points and ideas. 'Blessing' is written in free verse; this allows the third-person narrator to make expressive points with run-on lines, etc. Braithwaite uses couplets of varying length; however one is broken to emphasise the uncle's 'shattered' life and his obsession with his last carved piece – Ogun.

Question Bank 64
Poets in the English Literary Heritage

1 Remember that you only have 30 minutes; try to use brief, integrated quotations. Of course, your choice will be guided by personal preference. Two interesting poems to write about are 'Valentine' and 'War Photographer'. In 'Valentine' Duffy's first-person narrator argues that a lowly onion can be taken as a powerful symbol of love. The narrator confidently argues her case using the form best suited for conversation and argument: free verse. Try to explain the striking comparisons and sensual imagery that the narrator uses to persuade us. Are you convinced by Duffy's comparisons that an onion can be accepted as a token of love?

The third-person narrator of 'War Photographer' compares the photographer to 'a priest'. The photographer feels a sacred duty to act as a witness for the death and suffering that he found abroad. 'His editor will pick out five or six (photographs) for Sunday's supplement'. Although his photographs initially move readers, they are quickly forgotten. Why do you think this is so? The narrator's tone for the photographer is one of respect and admiration; what does the narrator's change of tone imply about

the editor and readers? The poem is narrated in the present tense for greater dramatic impact; its form of four stanzas of varying length reflects the cyclical pattern of the photographer's unusual job. At the beginning he arrives to develop his photographs; at the end he flies out to make new ones. But do we really care about what he brings us?

2 The two best poems to choose for this question are 'War Photographer' and 'Stealing'. Comment on the different styles of narration and how they reveal the character in each poem; the third-person narrator admires the photographer's work but ironically criticises the public; the first-person narrator in 'Stealing' speaks in a defensive, self-justifying, jerky manner as if he or she is giving an interview; both feel misunderstood. The 'Sunday supplement' readers do not really feel deeply enough about the photographs that he brings back from war-torn countries and the thief ends the interview with: 'You don't understand a word I'm saying, do you?' Both characters seem anonymous. However, the thief is even more ambiguous as the thief could be of any age and of either sex.

Comment on the contrasting characters of the photographer and the thief: the first is socially minded, the second exhibits anti-social behaviour. Nevertheless, each poem explores the motives of the figure. Notice how each character shares highly-developed visual skills: the photographer needs these to frame his pictures and the thief uses them to remember what he or she has stolen. Notice the striking description

of the snowman:
'Midnight. He looked magnificent; a tall, white mute beneath the winter moon.'

Poems from Other Cultures and Traditions

1 Good choices here would be 'Half-Caste' by John Agard and 'Nothing's Changed' by Tatamkhulu Africa. Both poems embody protest as a theme. Agard's first-person narrator argues that the unthinking use of the term 'half-caste' can lead its speakers into the prejudice of seeing people of mixed race as only half human. The poem's ironic tone undermines the usage of the term as the narrator makes a number of unusual though persuasive comparisons from painting, music and the weather to prove his case. He deliberately uses West Indian dialect to counter the standard English term, 'half-caste'. Free verse is an appropriate form for an argumentative poem that is phonetically spelled and uses no punctuation; the repetition of 'explain yuself' exemplifies the poem's tone. 'Nothing's Changed' is a protest poem that registers the frustration of its first-person narrator, who finds that South Africa after apartheid remains much the same. Towards the end of the poem the narrator feels as if he is returning to his boyhood when he sees that the whites still 'squat' on formerly black land in Cape Town's District Six. Only this time it is an expensive, smart new inn with a 'guard at its gatepost' where the expected customers are rich white people. 'Down the road' men like the narrator eat cheap 'bunny chows' in a 'working man's café'. The sight of the inn angers the narrator who sees that democracy has only legitimised the differences

that existed before apartheid ended. For he sees the inn as a 'Whites only inn.
No sign says it is:
But we know where we belong.'

2 Two good choices for this question are 'Search for my Tongue' by Sujata Bhatt and 'Presents from my Aunts in Pakistan' by Moniza Alvi. Each poem's first-person narrator feels troubled about their identity in England and engages in a search for their 'roots'. The narrator begins 'Search for my Tongue' in a conversational manner with, 'You ask me what I mean by saying I have lost my tongue'. She finds her 'mother tongue' again through voicing it in her dreams. The chanted Gujarati language displaces her 'foreign tongue' (English). The narrator celebrates the rediscovery of her identity by using an extended metaphor that compares her mother tongue to a 'flower' that regularly 'blossoms' out of her mouth.

The mixed race female first-person narrator of Moniza Alvi's poem rediscovers her Pakistani roots through wearing a *salwar kameez* and other brightly coloured items from Pakistan. Although initially reluctant to try on the *salwar kameez* she soon becomes 'aflame' and feels her 'roots' with, 'I couldn't rise up out of its fire'. The experience transforms the narrator's feelings about her 'roots' as she later reflects on how, as a baby, she 'sailed to England' from Pakistan. She also considers how the lives of her aunts and girls in Lahore are so different from hers. The use of free verse in each poem aids the poets' reflections as they search for their 'roots'. Alvi's poem visually represents the idea of

being 'caught between two cultures'.

Question Bank 65
1 true
2 false
3 false
4 true
5 true
6 true
7 true
8 false
9 true
10 false

Question Bank 66
1 reading
2 style
3 text
4 context
5 craft
6 genre

Question Bank 67
1 Any five of the following:
· characters
· dialogue
· narrators
· description, mood and atmosphere
· plots
· settings in the past, present or future as well as settings of place
· themes, ideas and messages.

2 Any five of the following:
· They are usually based on a specific incident or point in time.
· They have just one plot.
· Description needs to be far more concise.
· Description has to add meaning to every part of the story or plot.
· Striking details and images are used more often.
· Dialogue is shorter and more fragmented.
· Fewer characters must often do and say more in less time.

3 There is not enough space for many characters and there is usually just one plot.

4 The longer form means

that there is more space to develop several plots.

Question Bank 68
1 false
2 true
3 true
4 false
5 false
6 false
7 true
8 true

Question Bank 69
1 first person
2 third person
3 first person

Question Bank 70
1 conversation
2 description, variety
3 personalities
4 motives
5 see through
6 think
7 sympathy

Question Bank 71
Read again the list of techniques that writers use to create mood and atmosphere and look for these in the passage. Write about the effect that Stoker achieves using these techniques.

Question Bank 72
1 ideas, messages or issues
2 change; self-realisation and growing up; strained or failed relationships between generations; or any others that you have studied
3 change from innocence to experience; love and the social relationships between men and women; ideals and the corruption of power; racism and the importance of independence, roots and family – these are just some of the themes that you may come across
4 for greater understanding of your text
5 There is a lack of space to develop other themes.
6 reading and understanding

Question Bank 73

1 c
2 Any of the following:
- to quickly determine the text's main ideas
- to find facts quickly
- to find the topic sentence of each paragraph
- to understand information through chapter headings, main headings and subheadings
- to find and read carefully the last paragraph for summary information
- to find key information in tables, charts and boxes
- to ignore parts of texts that have unnecessary information
- to read exam texts and answer questions.
3 reading a whole text quickly to get an understanding of what it is about

Question Bank 74

a opinion
b fact
c opinion
d opinion
e opinion
f fact (this can be checked, although this fact may change)
g fact
h opinion
i fact
j fact

Question Bank 75

The type of text is an essay. However, writing of this kind is often presented as articles in newspapers. It aims to explain and describe Orwell's experience of shooting the elephant and the elephant's horribly slow death. The expected audience is the general public and especially anyone interested in the activities of the British in colonial countries in the 1930s and 1940s.

Question Bank 76

1 true
2 false
3 false
4 true
5 true
6 false

Question Bank 77

1 Use five to ten minutes to plan your answer. You could structure your answers by making all the points 'for' in the first half of your answer and the points 'against' in the second half. Remember to make your writing agree with your form: if you are writing a letter set it out with addresses, the date and give the appropriate ending. Use 'Yours sincerely' if you know the addressee and 'Yours faithfully' if you do not. The control that you have over your writing is most important. Avoid sounding pompous and foolishly outraged by using evidence to support your points; aim to use some of the techniques used for persuasive writing mentioned in the advertising section of this book. Check your work for standard English, punctuation, spelling and expression. Keep your intended audience in mind as well as your purpose and you will not go wrong.

2 Use five to ten minutes to plan your answer. Remember that your purpose is to explain or describe and you should do so as clearly as you can. You will possibly use several semi-colons in your piece for this type of writing. Your expression and use of punctuation will be important for this question so remember to leave five minutes to proofread your work. Examiners think that the quality of your writing is more important than the form in which you present it.

Question Bank 78

1 Punctuation is the system of marks that we use in writing to express ourselves and to clarify our meaning for others.
2 speech
3 tone, pauses and body language
4 posture, use of eyes, hands, elbows, legs, etc.
5 Mostly well after it is written.
6 To keep our meaning clear.

Question Bank 79

1 false
2 true
3 true
4 true
5 false
6 true
7 false
8 true
9 true

Question Bank 80

1 b
2 a
3 b
4 c
5 a

Question Bank 81

1 statement
2 question
3 exclamation
4 instruction
5 instruction
6 question
7 instruction
8 exclamation
9 question
10 rhetorical question

Question Bank 82

1 A clause is a group of words that includes a verb.
2 Sentences have at least one clause. They also have a punctuation mark to complete them.
3a it began to rain
b Amy's father bought her a new car
c I am spending half my life in Internet chat rooms!

4a as I love following all the characters' lives

b because she recognises the sound of my car

c after getting my Saturday job

5 after, as, since, because, if, etc.

Question Bank 83

1 false
2 true
3 true
4 false
5 false
6 false
7 true

Question Bank 84

1a When you go to the shops please buy me: three packets of chewing gum, two bags of cheese and onion crisps, a Mars Bar and a can of coke.

b 'It's too far to walk,' said Jade wearily. James replied, 'Come on Jade; it's only one more mile.'

c Stuart, who is five years younger than Sam, is the baby of the family.

2a They separate words, phrases and connectives in sentences.

b They separate items in a list.

c They clarify sentences that would otherwise be misleading.

3 At the end of a sentence (and usually not before *and*).

Question Bank 85

1 :

2a Can I have: two cheese sandwiches, a slice of gateau, a cup of coffee and two serviettes please? (The sentence would still be correct without the colon, but it helps the reader.)

b A colon is needed after 'vain' before the quotation.

c Krystle worked hard for her exams: she got four A*s and four As.

3 before lists; to introduce separated quotations; before quoted speech and before explanations

Question Bank 86

1a Both sides were equally drawn; it was one-one at half time.

b The twins have different personalities; Bianca loves talking and Alan hardly says a word.

c To err is human; to forgive, divine.

2

a I rose at 7am; I ate a full breakfast; I then got the car out of the garage and went to work.

b Go on holiday and enjoy yourselves; we will look after the house.

c It was a very cold night; the cat looked anxiously at the door.

3 To get to the ice rink: take the first turn on your left at Sainsburys; go half-way up Treetop Hill; go left at the traffic lights by the Red Lion and you're there.

Question Bank 87

1 inverted (upside-down) commas – 'x' or "x"
2 Remain consistent.
3 inverted commas
4 Use inverted commas around titles.
5 Use italics and then there is no need for inverted commas.
6 Proofread it to check for inverted commas.

Question Bank 88

1 b
2 a
3 b
4 a
5 b

Question Bank 89

1 false
2 true
3 true
4 true
5 true
6 a and c

Question Bank 90

1 That letters are missing in words or phrases.

2 in dialect; when writing the time; in lines of poetry; in plays or novels for direct speech

3a What's the matter? Don't you feel well?

b We'd have gone to the party if they'd asked us to come.

c Let's get cracking because we've got a lot to do.

d It's time to give the cat its medicine. (The second *its* is the possessive pronoun.)

Question Bank 91

1 place
2 topic
3 speaker
4 speaker
5 topic
6 time
7 topic

Question Bank 92

Use the spelling method that best suits you to learn any spellings that you do not know.

Scoring grid

Glossary

Accent the sound someone makes as they pronounce their vowels and consonants

Alliteration the repetition of consonants for an effect. For example, 'friendly fingers'

Analyse to unravel

Assonance the repetition of vowel sounds for an emphasis, etc. For instance, 'the merciless iced east winds that knive us.' W. Owen

Blank verse unrhymed poetic lines of Shakespeare's plays

Caesura any kind of punctuation that punctuates a line in poetry

Clichés overused expressions such as 'blue print' or 'unveil'

Clause groups of words that include a verb; they can stand on their own as a sentence

Couplet a two-line stanza of poetry

Connectives words that join writing together, such as 'and' and 'although'

Dependent clauses clauses that cannot stand on their own as sentences. For instance, *'After scoring the winning goal'*

Diction the poet or author's word choices

Direct speech spoken words set out as writing

Dramatic monologue usually spoken by a single speaker of a poem

Emotive language words and phrases intended to move audiences to sympathise or empathise

Enjambment or run-on lines lines which run-on within stanzas and between stanzas in poetry for an effect

Facts and opinion facts can be checked and proved; opinions cannot

Fiction made-up writing

Non-fiction not made-up

First person narrator a character from within a story tells it

Free verse lines and stanzas of varying length in poetry

Genre type or kind of writing such as 'detective novels'

Historical context what was happening during the time when a text was written

Imagery figures of speech such as similes, metaphors, puns, etc.

Independent clauses main clauses that can stand on their own to form a sentence. 'After scoring the winning goal *he celebrated the victory with his friends.'*

Local dialect informal speech such as Cockney for friends and family

Metaphor	an image and a strong comparison using or implying 'is,' 'am' or 'are'. For instance, 'The eagle-eyed boy never missed a trick'
Montage	rapid editing in movies. Fast-changing images
Narrative	writing or speaking that tells a story
Onomatopoeia	words that sound like their meaning. For example, 'pop', 'crackle' and 'rustle'
Orals	three assessed talks that you must give in front of your teacher
Personification	(person-making) a powerful metaphor in which something that is not human is given human feelings or characteristics. For instance, 'The sun smiled', 'the moon sighed' and 'the grass whispered'
Plot	the outline and main events of a story
Poetic verse	rhymed poetry
Phrases	groups of words of two or more without verbs. For example, 'chalk and cheese'
Prose	ordinary speech in writing
Quatrain	a four-line stanza of poetry
Received pronunciation	an accent picked up in some public schools

Rhetorical questions	questions that prompt others to agree with you
Rhythm	the sound and pace of lines of poetry
Scanning	means locating precise pieces of information in texts
Sentences	groups of words that include a clause that begin with a capital letter and are completed by full stops, semi-colons, colons and question marks
Similes	an image and a comparison using 'as' or 'like'. For example, 'She's like a witch'
Skimming	means reading over a text quickly to get its gist
Standard English	a dialect of English for formal communication with people that you may not know
Text	anything written or filmed
Theme	a message or a main idea in a text
Third-person narrator	the narrator views events from outside the story
Tone	the attitude of a writer to their topic/audience
Topic sentence	the main sentence in a paragraph
Topic word	the main word in a topic sentence

Useful websites

General

http://www.bbc.co.uk/education/gcsebitesize/   *Excellent*

http://www.apclarke.freeserve.co.uk/index.htm

http://www.s-cool.co.uk/   *An excellent site for both GCSE and A-level*

http://www.learn.co.uk/default.asp?WCI=Home

http://www.english-teaching.co.uk/

http://www.gosford-hill.oxon.sch.uk/etuk/etuk.htm

http://www.homeworkhigh.co.uk/

http://www.pinkmonkey.com

http://www.revise.it/reviseit/

http://www.shunsley.eril.net/armoore/contents.html#ks4   *Outstanding!*

http://www.sparknotes.com

Media Sites

http://www.filmeducation.org/

http://www.media-awareness.ca/eng/med/class/teamedia/tujs.htm

Shakespeare Sites worth a visit

http://www.dnaco.net/~aleed/corsets/   *Elizabethan costumes, etc.*

http://renaissance.dm.net/compendium/home.html   *Brilliant for historical detail*

http://www.renfaire.com/Language/index.html

http://www.shakespeare-online.com/

http://shakespeare.palomar.edu/playcriticism.htm

http://stjohns-chs.org/english/shakespeare/Shindex.html

Story Sites

http://atoledo.freeyellow.com/stories.html

http://www.cityofshadows.stegenga.net/ghoststories.html

Index

First published in Great Britain in 2002 by Virgin Books Ltd and Letts Educational Ltd

Virgin Books Ltd
Thames Wharf Studios
Rainville Road
London
W6 9HA

Letts Educational Ltd
Chiswick Centre
414 Chiswick High Road
London
W4 5TF

A catalogue record for this book is available from the British Library.

ISBN 0 7535 0658 0

Prepared by *specialist* publishing services, Milton Keynes
Printed and bound in Great Britain by Clays, Suffolk

Letts Educational Ltd is a division of Granada Learning Ltd, part of the Granada Group.